Give Life to Your DREAMS

8 Principles for a Happy Life

RICARDO BENTANCUR

Pacific Press®
Publishing Association

Nampa, Idaho | Oshawa, Ontario, Canada
www.pacificpress.com

Cover design by Gerald Lee Monks
Cover design resources from iStockphoto/Yobro10
Inside design by Aaron Troia

The author assumes full responsibility for the accuracy of all facts and quotations as cited in this book.

You can obtain additional copies of this book by calling toll-free 1-800-765-6955 or by visiting http://www.adventistbookcenter.com.

Library of Congress Cataloging-in-Publication Data

Names: Bentancur, Ricardo, author.
Title: Give life to your dreams : 8 principles for a happy life / Ricardo Bentancur.
Description: Nampa : Pacific Press Publishing Association, 2017.
Identifiers: LCCN 2017003636 | ISBN 9780816362530 (pbk.)
Subjects: LCSH: Happiness—Religious aspects—Christianity. | Conduct of life.
Classification: LCC BV4647.J68 B46 2017 | DDC 248.4—dc23 LC record available at
    https://lccn.loc.gov/2017003636

February 2017

Give Life to Your
DREAMS

This book is dedicated to four persons with whom I unexpectedly crossed paths in life and who played a positive role in my destiny: Pastor Luis Pérez, Pastor José Tabuenca, Dr. Miguel Valdivia, and Dr. Bob Kyte.

The fact that you are happy you owe to God;

the fact that you continue feeling that way,

you owe to yourself.

—J. Melton

Contents

Introduction

Is there any meaning to the pursuit of happiness in this life?

I always remember the response made by the famous Mexican-American actor Anthony Quinn to a question put to him by an Argentine reporter as the celebrity stepped off his plane in Buenos Aires: "Are you happy?" Back then, in my early youth (around the year 1981), the question seemed a bit trivial and the response clever: "Happy are the fools."

But today, with the passing of the years, and in counterposition to my Spanish blood always holding happiness suspect, I have come to consider that question anything but silly. And neither do I believe that only fools are happy, despite the witty line expressed by Quinn, whose Latin blood flowed passionately through his veins like hot lava from a volcano. His off-the-cuff expression runs contrary to the thinking of the country that gave a resting place to his mortal remains—the only country in the world whose Constitution proclaims the right of all its people to the "pursuit of happiness."

Not long ago I came across several scientific studies that conclude that only 10 percent of our contentment depends on the pleasurable circumstances and pleasant situations that surround us. You may be aware that when scientists seek to establish the percentage of genetic and environmental factors acting in a particular human phenomenon, they turn to twins as their control specimens. Well, recent studies conducted on twins have found that 50 percent of happiness comes "prepackaged" in the genes and is not dependent on external pleasures such as traveling, winning the lottery, or your favorite football team winning the Super Bowl. This "reference value," or initial set point, cannot be altered; it is an invariable constant. What can be altered is the remaining 40 percent, a margin of happiness that is important because it depends on what each one of us does, on our efforts to increase our happiness in a lasting way.

What shall we do with this 40 percent that we have in our power in order to improve our lives?

This is precisely what this book is about. Based on recent empirical studies of medicine and positive psychology, we will track the path that leads to wholistic well-being, which we can call happiness. These scientific findings are probably the most significant achievements of psychology in recent times. They prompted Dr. Sonja Lyubomirsky to develop "strategies" by which every human being can be happy. What is surprising is that these "strategies" were already present in the life of Jesus and are incorporated into His principles of life.

Each chapter in this book presents a principle of life and is divided into six sections: (1) a true story, (2) what science says (thanks to Dr. Mario Pereyra for his help in this area), (3) what the Bible says, (4) how to integrate the principle in question into our lives, (5) the teachings that the Bible offers us (thanks to Pastor Julio Chazarreta for the development of these biblical studies), and (6) an assessment to see how we stand in relation to the principle of life studied in each chapter.

I invite you to join me on the road to happiness through the pages of this little book.

Chapter 1

Gratitude

Gratitude is not only the greatest of virtues,
but the parent of all others.
—Marcus Tullius Cicero

It was a dark, frigid night in January 2004. I had crossed the border to visit a sick woman, the mother of one of the farmworkers who pick vegetables in Yuma, Arizona. After the visit, I walked to the bus stop to wait for my ride back to the "line" in order to reenter the United States (US). A few minutes after I reached the bus stop, a Volkswagen van pulled over a few yards in front of me and then took off again. It sped around the block and this time hit the brakes right in front of me. Out jumped two hooded men, who grabbed me at gunpoint and without a word shoved me inside the vehicle. In an instant my life drastically changed: I found myself blindfolded, lying on the cold floor of the van, choking on dust in the midst of the most nauseating odors.

Kidnapped. I don't know whether you have ever had a gun pressed to your temple. It is a moment that escapes time. Everything seems compressed into the swirling present. You feel like a drowning victim flailing in the waves and see your entire life pass by as if in a feature-length film crammed into mere seconds. At that moment I experienced absolute impotence. Someone else was in charge of my body and intended to take charge of my mind as well, intimidating me, evoking fear, perhaps the most destructive of emotions. I was left with my fragmented thoughts; I offered no resistance. I simply could not control the actions for which I was not responsible.

The van shortly left pavement behind and entered a rough dirt road filled with potholes. My body bounced like a sack of potatoes, and I could hardly breathe; the air was thick with dust coming through the slits of the beat-up, old Volkswagen. After traveling what, to my mind, seemed like an interminable distance, the vehicle came to a stop. I could barely hear the men mulling something over among themselves. Immediately the van was in motion again, and after traveling a relatively short distance, the one guarding me told me to get out, keep my eyes closed, and stand facing a wall. I was not to look one way or the other, or I would be a dead man. Next I heard the squeal of tires as they pealed out, leaving me standing there alone.

I stood still, staring at the wall, for a few tense seconds, and then I looked nervously both ways, seeing nothing more than a dog crossing the dusty street. A block or so away there was a street lamp, so I walked in the direction of the light. My body was shaking, perhaps from the cold but more likely from the emotion and relief of still having a living body! I approached a house and knocked on the door. A man opened the door, and I told him what had just happened to me. The good man apologized to me as if he had been an accomplice to the event. But, of course, he was not; he was simply embarrassed about what had happened to an undeserving stranger visiting his town. He was thoughtful and gracious, as are many folks living along the border. They are honest, hardworking people who look for a better tomorrow and who want to live out their dreams. He offered to take me in his car back to the "line," and about an hour later I finally crossed back to the US side.

I did not understand at that time what had happened or why. Often, the first question that comes to one's mind after going through a traumatic experience is, why me? You have to allow time for the answer to unfold. And, even then, some things might never be revealed in this life. At any rate, I continued visiting Yuma during the following years to preach the Word of God to the field-workers and to leave them with that great Book of hope. I always carry a supply of Bibles to offer people. And I continued crossing the border. For more than a quarter of a century I have dedicated time each year to this ministry and frequently cross back and forth over the border.

One early January evening in 2009, when I was finishing my day's work among the field-workers, a tall, well-built young man approached me and said, "Father, I owe you a debt of gratitude."

Many people call me "Father," as if I were a priest; although I have explained many times that I am a father but only to my two daughters. I figured on this occasion that he was simply another person who had ordered a Bible but hadn't yet gotten around to paying. Then, I sensed that this was something more serious, because the young fellow's lower lip was trembling; he could barely speak he was so nervous.

"A long time ago, you attended my grandmother's funeral, and I met you there. I also worked for Oseguera and remember you coming to minister among us workers."

I could not remember exactly who he might be, but I listened as he continued: "At that time I was into drugs. At one time several of us set out to get money, and we saw you. When we grabbed you at that bus stop, I did not recognize who you were. But during that ride in the van, I could not help but feel that you were someone I had seen before. Finally it came to me that you were the Father who had officiated at my grandmother's funeral."

My mind was racing and spinning like in the van. He continued with his confession: "Two years ago I bought a Bible from you while I was working for the Garcia family, and that was when I started attending a Christian church. They helped me escape from drugs. I attend church every week, and all this time I kept thinking about you. Last year I saw you when you came to bring Bibles to the workers, but I did not have the courage to say anything to you. Today I told myself that I would not wait any longer. I want to apologize to you for what I did and to thank you for officiating at my grandmother's funeral and especially for selling me that Bible."

I was stunned, and I only managed to say, "I receive your gratitude as a gift. Your gratitude is worth much more than all your mistakes."

Life always gives us the opportunity to give and to receive. That was the moment to receive.

What does science say about gratitude?

Science has shown that gratitude is vital to rebuilding life and to being happy.

Gratitude garnered little attention from psychology until investigations during the past decade placed it onstage as one of the most important "strengths of character."[1] Psychological research has found abundant evidence of the benefits of gratitude upon both physical and mental health.[2] An investigation found that the most grateful people show higher levels of satisfaction with life, are more outgoing and optimistic, cultivate positive emotions, and report less depression and lower stress levels compared to others.[3] In addition, it was found that gratitude raises levels of self-esteem, not only for the short term but also for the long term.[4] And grateful people have lower levels of neuroticism, or emotional imbalances, because they do not feed on frustrations.[5] Other studies found that gratitude improves human relationships and generates better social integration and satisfaction with life.[6]

Perhaps the research with the most impact related to gratitude was the research that was carried out by Danner and colleagues,[7] who studied a group of 678 nuns for more than sixty years, conducting retrospective monitoring and periodic evaluations. They found that the nuns who at the age of twenty revealed gratitude and other positive emotions lived almost ten years longer and did not suffer from Alzheimer's disease compared to those who were unhappy and unthankful. This study continued even after the nuns passed away: their brains were examined, and it was found that they contained none of the characteristics related to Alzheimer's, and those who bore a predisposition to the disease never suffered from its symptoms.[8]

Gratitude is the first secret to being happy.

Jesus and gratitude

He was a foreigner. His gaze, like that of every man in a foreign land, always sought permission or perhaps offered apologies. His eyes expressed the debt that one feels within his own soul when he finds himself in an unknown land.

But this man, besides being a stranger, carried on his flesh the marks of death, which drew looks from those who saw him not just as a foreigner but also as a risk to their own lives. He had come to Jerusalem from Samaria with goods to sell. That night he did not know where to go, and like so many who do not know where they are going, he got carried along by winds that too frequently lead to misfortune. So he sought entertainment at one of the hovels in town to also satisfy his sexual desires.*

A few days into that trip to self-destruction, he awoke in a sweat. It was very hot, but he noticed his face and torso were covered with grainy sores, which caused him to itch. And he started to scratch them to calm the itching, but nothing alleviated it. Soon those sores spread all over his body and turned into bleeding ulcers, which acquired a reddish hue. Under these conditions, he could no longer return home to Samaria.

With mounting desperation he asked for help, but no one could help him. Finally, he went to the priest, as instructed in Leviticus chapter 13. The priest determined that the Samaritan had leprosy. He imposed on him a distinctive tunic, gave him a small warning bell, and confined him to the depths of a valley, to some caves where lepers dwelt at a safe distance from the general population. From that moment on, his life changed categorically: the bustle of commerce, the nights of partying—everything came to a stop. He found himself isolated on the outskirts of society.

With the passing of the months, the silence stirred up the memories and remorse: *What will become of my family?*

Nostalgia and tearful sorrow racked his soul. He had heard from his companions in the same misfortune about a Teacher from Nazareth who cured every type of disease. He did not know whether he wanted to be healed from his disease so much as he wanted to receive healing for his soul. When they

---

* This inference, which is not explicit in the biblical account, arises from the fact that serious scientific studies claim that the "leprosy" of Jesus' time could have been a form of syphilis. Scientists do not confirm as fact that the leprosy known by medical science today in China and India is the same as the one mentioned in the Bible.

spoke to him of the Great Physician, his entire being shuddered with sacred trembling.

One day the ten lepers saw, at a distance, Jesus and His disciples. They shouted in desperate unison: " 'Jesus, Master, have mercy on us.' When he saw them he said, 'Go and show yourselves to the priests.' And as they went along, they were cleansed" (Luke 17:13, 14, NET). It was the miracle he had dreamed of! As he ran, the sores began to heal, and his face, hands, and body were covered with soft skin like that of a child. A deep feeling of appreciation filled his soul. As soon as the priest certified his healing, he returned joyfully, shouting to every passerby that Jesus had healed him and glorifying God. And upon arriving where the Master was, "he fell with his face to the ground at Jesus' feet and thanked him. . . . Then Jesus said, 'Were not ten cleansed? Where are the other nine? Was no one found to turn back and give praise to God except this foreigner?' Then he said to the man, 'Get up and go your way. Your faith has made you well' " (verses 16–19, NET).

The gratitude felt by this healed leper came from the deepest layers of his soul. He once again thanked and praised God, not so much because the sores on his skin had disappeared but because the wounds deep down in his soul were healed. Gratitude has its firmest foundation in God, who is no respecter of persons. The leper was a foreigner, a man without rights, and therefore he grasped in a way that none of the Jewish lepers could the unprejudiced graciousness of that miracle. In addition to being physically healed of his leprosy, the Samaritan felt fully accepted by God. Gratitude comes from the awareness of such acceptance.

The why and how of practicing gratitude

The writer Otto F. Bollnow says that there is no other indicator so adequate for determining the inner spiritual and moral health of an individual than the ability to feel gratitude.[9]

I have been married to my wife, Florencia, for more than forty years. During all these decades, she has always, without missing a single day, prepared and served me the best food. I remember when we were young newlyweds, she would hurry home from work during her lunchtime to prepare me the most healthy and appetizing food. After eating with me, she would return to her job to finish the day. She did this for many years. Now I must confess something, and I am ashamed to say it: during these forty years I assumed her loving gesture was merely the fulfillment of her marital duty. How horrible! Sometimes I thanked her for her efforts, but I never fully understood the meaning of the words *thank you* until recently, when I started writing this book and began looking more deeply into the value of gratitude. Can you believe this?

Yesterday, as we sat down to the tasty and healthy meal she placed on the table for us, I said, "Thank you, Florencia, thank you very much." It seems that my "thank you" had a more meaningful impact for her, because she responded, "Thanks be to God and to your work, which make it all possible." She was really saying, "Your love and recognition are worth more than everything else you can do for me." We can say that gratitude is the heart's fond memory. In thinking about the power of this virtue, it occurred to me that it brings into balance our giving and receiving—the balance of love. And I also thought about the power it has to establish or reconcile an emotional relationship. The essence of gratitude is to inaugurate a relationship of love and life.

Gratitude is the mother of all virtues, of all the secrets of happiness, of all the possibilities in human relationship, because in saying "thank you," we recognize that the *other* has bestowed on us a gift. I recognize my neighbor, but sometimes because of proximity and familiarity I take too much for granted and fail to consider just who my neighbor is! When I say "thank you" to Florencia, I acknowledge that I accept her appetizing creations as a gift of her grace. It is more than the recognition of her marital duty. When I express my gratitude to her for something, I recognize that what I receive has a far greater value than what I can pay. Many times I have told my wife: "This plate of food cannot be paid for with Visa," recalling the advertising from that credit card that said the card could pay for anything except the most dazzling value of the spirit, which is love.

Moreover, people who know how to receive the words *thank you* from another broaden their spirit, because they feed on that recognition and have the energy to keep giving. The exchange relationship is not severed. In contrast, an indifferent, self-centered person cuts short the cycle of life. The self-centered person does not understand that "none of us lives to himself, and none dies to himself" (Romans 14:7, WEB). Remember that life is a great chain of mutual aid. Notice how the sun invigorates at its rising and the streams of water refresh at their passing; and we have fresh air to breathe. The wife helps when she prepares the bread, the husband when he works, or vice versa. As friends we lend each other a hand; on the job we team up for mutual benefit at our various posts of service and responsibility. We all help in the chain of life. He who knows how to give will receive. And he who knows how to receive will give.

Gratitude is not a simple act fulfilled with a verbalized "thank you"; it is a way of being, an attitude of life. Therefore, gratitude must begin with God, the Giver of life. When we get up in the morning with health and express in our hearts and on our lips a word of gratitude to the Creator, the darkness dissipates as the wind carries the dark clouds away. In his exhortation to gratitude, the psalmist David says: "Make a joyful noise unto the LORD, all the earth" (Psalm 100:1, MEV).

Every day we should thank our parents, who gave us life. In giving us life, they essentially gave us everything. From our birth we are ultimately responsible for our destiny. People who do not have a word of appreciation for their parents, despite what type of parents they might have been, are bound to their past. Failure feeds off frustration, and frustration feeds on the inability to grasp that we are the builders of our own destiny. Out of ungratefulness to their parents, many do not mature or find meaning in their own lives. They live as neurotic people.

Gratitude makes us historians of the benignity of the past; not of the misfortunes.

We should express gratitude to our spouse every day to preserve that delicate balance between giving and receiving. We receive love in order to give love. If we do not give, we will not receive, and the exchange is severed. Only if this balance is achieved will there be any possibility of delving deeper into the cycle of life. Therefore, the word of the wise to spouses is: "May you be captivated by her love always" (Proverbs 5:19, NET). Gratitude re-creates the relationship between giving and receiving.

There can be no peace in the married life if the one receiving does not give something in return that goes beyond the mere "fulfillment of duty." He who loves gives much more than what simple reciprocity demands.

In like manner, when one demands more than what the other can give, the exchange wears out. For example, think about this: when someone has been unfaithful to their spouse, and the latter plants themselves in their innocence, they prevent their partner from bringing remedy the situation. If the victim considers themselves too noble and does not accept their own dark and evil side, there can be no amends. So then, the relationship is destroyed. For there to be a deep relationship of exchange, we need to come out of even what we consider just. But everything has a limit. This introduces us to the theme of forgiveness, which we will discuss in the next chapter.

Give thanks for everything. For bright days and for dark days. For adversities and for adversaries. Because they also teach us.

The Bible Teaching: Jesus and Gratitude
(Luke 17:11–19)

Introduction

Why did Jesus heal the ten lepers when He knew that only one would return to thank Him? In the Bible, the number ten is a symbol of completeness. Jesus healed ten as an expression of His love for humanity and His power to save all sinners who come to Him, as did those lepers (John 3:16). Have you ever felt lost? Do you remember how you felt? What were your thoughts? How did you feel when you found the way? What relationship exists between being lost and leprosy?

Let's study what the Bible says about sin and salvation:

What does God compare leprosy to? *(Isaiah 1:4–6)*

The Bible compares leprosy to sin, which casts us away from the glory of God. That is to say, without God, we are lost (see Romans 3:23).

What can we do to solve our problem of sin? *(Jeremiah 2:22)*

We can do nothing, which means we are in need of a Savior.

What was Jesus' mission on earth? *(Luke 19:10)*

Jesus is our Savior. He cleanses us from the leprosy of sin.

What did Jesus do to save us? *(Romans 3:24, 25)*

The life and death of Jesus guarantees our salvation and our cleansing. That blessing is available to us all.

How can I receive that cleansing and forgiveness? *(1 John 1:9)*

"To confess our sins" means to give ourselves to God, to accept our condition, and to recognize His power to save and redeem us.

What is God's attitude toward us? *(Matthew 11:28; Isaiah 1:18)*

God invites us to come to Him just as we are so that He can cleanse us completely. We must go to Him with our burden of sin, because only in Him can we find redemption.

Why did Christ relate the gratitude of the leper to his faith?
(Ephesians 2:8)

When we understand that God has saved us by His grace through faith, which is a gift from Him, we cannot but acknowledge it with praise and worship to Him (see Psalm 100:1).

Conclusion

Jesus healed the lepers to show His power to cleanse our lives from sin. By His blood we are forgiven, cleansed, saved, restored, and at peace with God. A Chinese proverb says: "When you drink water, remember its source."

An appeal

Will you accept God's invitation to come to Jesus and receive His forgiveness and the cleansing He offers you?

Resolution

I accept Jesus and His grace in my heart in order to be saved through Him.

I sign this in acceptance: _____.

How Grateful Am I?
Evaluation of Gratitude

Place an *X* in the column that best expresses your personal gratitude beside each one of the statements, specifying the degree of agreement or application to your case with the corresponding number, according to the explanation below.

1. *Absolutely agree.* It applies fully to my way of thinking.
2. *Agree.* It applies for the most part to my way of thinking.
3. *Slightly agree.* It only partially applies to my way of thinking.
4. *Neutral.* I am neither for nor against this way of thinking.
5. *Slightly disagree.* It barely applies to my way of thinking.
6. *Disagree.* It does not generally apply to my way of thinking.
7. *Strongly disagree.* It does not apply at all to my way of thinking.

Statements	1	2	3	4	5	6	7
1. I have much to be grateful for in life.							
2. If I were to make a list of all the things and people that I am thankful for, the list would be very long.							
3. When I see the world in which I live, I do not see much to be grateful for.							
4. I am grateful to many people.							
5. As I mature, I value more the people, events, and situations that have formed part of the story of my life.							
6. I can go for long periods of time without feeling that I need to be thankful to someone about something.							

Interpretation for the evaluation of gratitude

1. For questions 1, 2, 4, and 5, score your answer according to this scale: If you answered 1, it is worth 7 points; and subsequently 2 = 6; 3 = 5; 4 = 4; 5 = 3; 6 = 2; and 7 = 1.

2. For questions 3 and 6, the scores correspond to the numbers above the columns.

3. Add up the results of the six answers. The results are as follows:

Gratitude

Results

7–24 points: very ungrateful
25–33 points: ungrateful
34–39 points: average
40, 41 points: very grateful
42 points: completely grateful

1. Christopher Peterson and Martin E. P. Seligman, *Character Strengths and Virtues: A Handbook and Classification* (Washington, DC: American Psychological Association, 2004).

2. Robert A. Emmons and Michael E. McCullough, *The Psychology of Gratitude* (Oxford: Oxford University Press, 2004).

3. Michael E. McCullough, Robert A. Emmons, and Jo-Ann Tsang, "The Grateful Disposition: A Conceptual and Empirical Topography," *Journal of Personality and Social Psychology* 82, no. 1 (January 2002): 112–127, doi: 10.1037/0022-3514.82.1.112.

4. Joshua A. Rash, M. Kyle Matsuba, and Kenneth M. Prkachin, "Gratitude and Well-Being: Who Benefits the Most From a Gratitude Intervention?" *Applied Psychology: Health and Well-Being* 3, no. 3 (November 2011): 350–369, doi: 10.1111/j.1758-0854.2011.01058.x.

5. Peterson and Seligman, *Character Strengths and Virtues*.

6. Jeffrey J. Froh, Giacomo Bono, and Robert Emmons, "Being Grateful Is Beyond Good Manners: Gratitude and Motivation to Contribute to Society Among Early Adolescents," *Motivation and Emotion* 34, no. 2 (June 2010): 144–157, doi: 10.1007/s11031-010-9163-z.

7. Deborah D. Danner, David A. Snowdon, and Wallace V. Friesen, "Positive Emotions in Early Life and Longevity: Findings From the Nun Study," *Journal of Personality and Social Psychology* 80, no. 5 (May 2001): 804–813, doi: 10.1037/0022-3514.80.5.504.

8. Gary R. Collins, "Revisiting the Nun Study," People Builder's Blog, May 4, 2010, https://peoplebuilder.wordpress.com/2010/05/04/382-revisiting-the-nun-study/.

9. Otto Friedrich Bollnow, *Filosofía de la esperanza: El problema de la superación del existencialismo* (Buenos Aires: Compañía General Fabril Editora, 1962).

Chapter 2

Forgiveness

In life we only learn to forgive when simultaneously
we come to see how much we need to be forgiven.
—Jacinto Benavente

On the corner of Pedro Campbell and Palmar Streets, just half a block from my house, lived the neighborhood pharmacist. He was a middle-aged man, tall and lanky, with an austere face. Every Sunday he left his home early, with a Bible tucked under his arm, headed to church, accompanied by his wife, Francisca. They passed in front of my house to catch the bus on Rivera Avenue that would drop them off in front of María Auxiliadora Catholic Church. During my childhood, there were few churches in our city. In fact, Montevideo is the only capital city in Latin America whose main square has no cathedral. It seems my countrymen are not very fervent Catholics. But that is not what this story is about. Rather, it is about those walks to the bus stop, when Francisca trailed along behind her husband at a short distance, just far enough behind to give the impression that she was only playing the role of accompanying her husband. The firm and direct footsteps of the man left no doubt as to who wore the pants in that marriage. It was what he had been taught in church: "Woman is man's ideal helpmeet." His companion, yes, but in the end, she was merely "the help." From childhood I perceived how misinterpreted a woman can be and how much contempt she has suffered in the history of civilization. Even in this country, gay rights seem to come before women's rights.

Francisca was extremely beautiful, if we can ever say that beauty has an "extreme." But what most caught my attention were her warm smile and her tender look, though sometimes sad, which were a sharp contrast with the cold aspect of her husband. Both worked at the pharmacy, located precisely at the intersection of Rivera and Campbell, but she was the one who gave the place an aroma of sweetness above the medicinal scents. I liked going to the drugstore when Francisca was there.

She respected her husband and loved him as far as he allowed. But—this is a reflection that I made many years later, when I had become an adult—her heart yearned for something more than her husband's protection or even his uprightness, which often seemed more of a vice than a virtue. I think that at the heart of that need lay the bitter seed that germinated in the events that I will now relate.

One morning, the neighborhood awoke to the wail of an ambulance that had been called to take the pharmacist to the hospital. A heart attack almost snatched away his life. What no one knew at the time, but later came to find out, was that Francisca had once cheated on her husband. He had caught her by surprise with her lover. What no one yet knew was that her husband, following his religious convictions, decided to remain with her and even to fight the good fight to forgive her. But he failed in the attempt. And in his helplessness he began to take bitter pleasure in hating his wife. He loved his hatred rather than her. He pretended that he had forgiven her in order to heap on punishment with a show of righteous mercy. Every time the pharmacist indulged this secret hatred, his heart died a little more, to the point that he almost didn't survive that morning's cardiac arrest.

Some weeks later a miracle took place. After recovering from his heart attack, the pharmacist returned to the neighborhood, but now everyone could see a marked change—he was jovial, happy, and apparently at peace in his heart. His face seemed to light up that old apothecary. Also, Francisca reflected her husband's newfound joy. Some neighbors said they had been "born again" and that the Angel of the Lord had visited the pharmacist one of those nights. Others mocked the idea of an angelic visit and came up with all kinds of ribald jokes at the expense of this couple. Even as a boy of about six or seven I sensed the tragedy of that man, but the change that came over him left me baffled.

In those years my mother was attending an evangelical church called Calvary Temple. One Wednesday evening during prayer meeting, I noticed the pharmacist and his wife seated a few pews from us. It seemed a little strange that they were attending this church, but what really piqued my curiosity was the figure of an "angel" sitting way in the back and seemingly observing all that was going on. I felt convinced that this "being" with long blond hair and a sweet, serene look must truly be the Angel of the Lord spoken of in the neighborhood. One Sunday, when the worship service ended, I told my mother that I was sure this mysterious being was Jesus and that he must be the one who had visited the pharmacist. But with one remark, my mother shot down my imaginative theological theory: "That is a woman you saw; she is the wife of the pastor." They were an American missionary couple.

Years have gone by. Not long ago I learned that elderly Francisca passed away in the arms of her beloved husband. I am now a middle-aged adult, and having accepted years ago the Christian faith, I understand many things now that my childhood heart found hard to comprehend. But still retaining my early gift for imagination, I would like to project how the dialogue might have gone between the pharmacist and the Angel of the Lord:

"There is only one remedy for your wounded heart: 'Take my advice and buy . . . from me white clothing so you can be clothed and your shameful nakedness will not be exposed, and buy eye salve to put on your eyes so you can see!' " (Revelation 3:18, NET).

The pharmacist needed eye drops so that he could see Francisca not as one who had betrayed him but as a vulnerable woman who needed him. Only a new way of seeing her through refreshed eyes could bring healing to the wounds of the past that gave him such pain. And only this miracle-touched vision could produce a better introspection of himself: the Angel had also advised him to buy "white clothes" to cover his own exposed shame.

I picture the pharmacist answering the Angel as follows:

"Nobody and nothing can change the past. Not even God can change it."

"Yes, wounded man, you're right," replied the Angel. "You cannot change the past, but you can heal the pain that it left you with. This can be done only by applying the divine eye drops."

"And how can I get those eye drops?"

"All you have to do is sincerely ask for them, and you will receive them. Then, every time you see Francisca through your new eyes, your heart will become stronger."

So the man's afflicted heart was finally convinced, and he pled for the divine eye drops that the Angel had promised. Very soon Francisca began to change in wonderful and mysterious ways before her husband's eyes. And not only in his eyes but also in her own inward-looking eyes as well. Together, they began a new life, thanks to that heavenly eye medicine.

The healing power of forgiveness

Forgiveness is the process of healing the wounds caused by serious offenses. Sometimes that process will require the help of health professionals, because one cannot travel that road alone. However, there is healing power in faith because it produces a "change of heart" toward the aggressor. Forgiving helps us overcome resentment and despair—the deathly opponents of forgiveness and hope—allowing love to gradually recover and trust to be restored. Forgiveness can lead to reconciliation, or not, according to the case. But it always implies a mysterious operation performed by the Holy Spirit in the human life. Correlational and experimental studies have shown that people who forgive have better physical and mental health, and consequently, they are happier.

An extensive bibliography gives an account of the latest scientific research connecting the power of forgiveness with the psychological processes, both individually and in interpersonal relationships. This is demonstrated in the development of personality[1] and in the effects on emotions,[2] such as in social relations,[3] matrimonial relationships,[4] filial relationships,[5] and relationships among friends and professionals.[6] However, the "impact of forgiveness on diseases and physical health remains largely unexplored, and the same regarding development of theoretical models that examine the relationship between forgiveness and physical health," reports Seybold.[7] For that reason, this scientist and his colleagues, set up a study involving sixty-eight volunteers, applying a scale of forgiveness—(self-forgiveness, forgiveness of others, and general forgiveness)—and correlated the results with different variables of the defense system of the body (e.g., hematocrit, cortisol, lipoproteins, cholesterol, triglycerides, white blood cells, T cells, and NK cells), psychopathology (e.g., anxiety, depression, anger, and hostility), and other psychological factors (stress and coping difficulties). The results found that high levels of forgiveness do relate to rates of good health in most immune system indicators studied (e.g., blood pressure, levels of lymphocytes, neutrophils, T cells, T-helper cells, B cells, NK cells, and the activity of T cells).

They also found that a high rate of forgiveness is associated with lower rates of smoking and alcoholism, due to the fact that people who are more forgiving are usually believers who also refrain from consuming illegal drugs.

Jesus and forgiveness

Chapter 8 of the Gospel of John recounts that one day Jesus was teaching in the temple courtyard when a woman caught in the act of adultery was dragged into His presence to be stoned. While writing out the sins of her accusers in the dust on the ground, Jesus said, "Let him who is without sin among you, be the first to throw a stone at her." The scheming men snuck away, shamed in their conscience. Then Jesus told the woman, "Neither do I condemn you. Go and sin no more" (John 8:3–11, MEV).

How was it that this woman came to the courtyard of the temple that morning? Imagine the case in the following context: She was a woman like Francisca, the wife of the pharmacist. She was married, and for that reason she was accused of adultery; it seems unlikely that she was a prostitute. And it is quite possible that she was also a victim of loneliness and the indifference of her husband. We might wonder whether he also was an adulterer. This woman was induced to sin through the old strategies of seduction. The discretion of the biblical account silences the details of the episode, and we as Christians would do well to show solidarity with that gesture. But one thing stands out: the woman was seduced into sin by those who were now accusing her.

A capture operation was mounted, and the lovers were caught by surprise. Suddenly, angry faces broke into the scene, and the men angrily shouted out her sins; they insulted her and harassed her to get dressed quickly. They pushed her toward the temple. No one concerned themselves with the scheme, with the man with whom she had committed adultery. She was the only evil and sinful one.

The secret fears of her heart, which had resisted so much that moment, bring her distress and blame. She keeps silent as in a daze she is led through the lavish halls of the temple, between gigantic columns of pearly marble, streaked with various colors. She crosses paths with ceremonial and solemn figures, who gaze at her with stern looks. She is taken before an altar where a prodigious elderly man is seated on a golden throne. The old man is wearing a miter on his head, with a golden badge on top of a blue sash, with the inscription "Holiness to the Lord."

An overwhelming silence fills the room. Then the sacrosanct verdict echoes the room: "My daughter, you have committed a very serious sin. You have disgraced the morality of the people and sinned against our sacred religion. You are a cursed woman! You must be stoned to death!"

The woman feels like lightning has struck her. Overcome, she collapses. She can only imagine a death by stoning. Then they lift her up by the arms and drag her once again through the halls of the temple out to the courtyard. When she raises her head, the rays of the morning sun practically blind her. Blinded by the glare, through half-closed eyes she sees the milling crowd and thinks: *There are my executioners, soon I will die. Thank You, Lord, for liberating me from this torture.*

But then there is a prolonged silence . . . not a murmur is heard.

What is happening? Why aren't they throwing stones at me? Are they going to judge me again? She dares to raise her eyes, and she beholds a kind and sympathetic face looking down at her. No one has ever looked at her this way! For the first time she feels recognized and appreciated. *Who is this Man? Why does everyone expect a response from Him? If the high priest said I must die, who is this Man to give His verdict?*

Unable to understand, she watches as Jesus begins to write in the dust of the ground the sins and evil plot of her accusers. Name by name, sin by sin. She looks at the words written in the dust, and she sees the effect those words

produce on the religious men: they all flee. She hears the calm voice of Jesus: "Woman, where are your accusers? Did no one condemn you?" Looking
around, she sees that no one is left, and she answers, "No one, Lord." Then
the Master's words descend on her ears like a balm of gentle grace and sweet
forgiveness: "Neither do I condemn you. Go, and sin no more" (John 8:2–11,
MEV).

Why and how to practice forgiveness

From where do we find the strength to forgive? Emotions cannot simply be
swept aside as by decree. Scars remain. But the wounds can stop bleeding
and begin to heal with forgiveness. Forgiveness is essentially an act of the
will, but the will must be illuminated and strengthened. We believers are
convinced that God's help is needed in order to produce the miracle of soft-
ening hearts hardened by resentment and to reach the blissful sensation of
liberation. Once we receive God's forgiveness for our wickedness, it becomes
easier for us to learn to forgive others. Jesus said, "Therefore I tell you, her
sins, which are many, are forgiven, for she loved much; but he who is forgiven
little, loves little" (Luke 7:47, RSV). The experience of receiving forgiveness
is what enables the recipient to grant it to others. Only then do the words of
the Lord's Prayer have meaning: "Father . . . forgive us . . . as we forgive our
debtors" (Matthew 6:9, 12, MEV). That is why the apostle Paul's advice to
us is: "Be kind to one another, tenderhearted, forgiving one another, even as
God in Christ forgave you" (Ephesians 4:32, NKJV).

The best representation of forgiveness in the Bible is the earthly sanctuary
and the heavenly sanctuary. The day Jesus died, the priest who officiated in the
atrium of the temple of Jerusalem was ready to offer the sacrificial lamb. But
when he raised the knife to kill the victim, the earth shook. Rattled, the priest
dropped the knife, and the lamb escaped. Immediately, the veil of the temple
was torn (see Matthew 27:51; *The Desire of Ages*, 756, 757). At the other end
of town, dark clouds hovered over the cross. When Jesus, the Passover Lamb
of God, exclaimed, "It is finished!" He died for the sins of the world. That
very event fulfilled the centuries-old ministry of the earthly sanctuary. The
Savior had completed His atoning sacrifice, and because the symbol had met
the reality, the rituals anticipating that sacrifice became obsolete. That fact
was dramatically revealed when the veil was torn and the lamb fled.

However, the story of salvation goes beyond the Cross. The resurrection
and ascension of Jesus directs our attention to the heavenly sanctuary, where
Christ, the slain Lamb of God, now takes on the priestly role. Since "Christ
was sacrificed once to take away the sins of many" (Hebrews 9:28, NIV), He
now makes the benefits of His atoning sacrifice available to all. This is divine

justice satisfied by sacrifice. This is what guarantees the divine forgiveness to humanity. The sacrifice of Christ is the price paid for forgiveness.

The New Testament reveals that Jesus now serves as High Priest "at the right hand of the throne of the Majesty of heaven," in the heavenly sanctuary. This sanctuary is the "true tabernacle, set up by the Lord, not by a mere human being" (Hebrews 8:1, 2, NIV). The heavenly sanctuary is not a metaphor. It is real. It is the primary dwelling place of God. It incorporates all three phases of Christ's ministry: (1) the substitutionary sacrifice, (2) the priestly mediation, and (3) the final judgment. It is the great work of righteous justice to ensure God's forgiveness to humanity.

This eternal truth was given to assure us that God forgives all of our sins, no matter how horrible they might have been, so that you also can forgive those who have offended you. But the most important question is this one: How do we practice forgiveness received from God toward those who have offended us?

Quite possibly you already know for yourself what I have written in the above paragraphs about how God's forgiveness for mankind works. And it is very likely that you, too, believe this and accept it in theory. That is not the difficult part. But what is truly hard for all of us is to take that forgiveness given to us freely from God and grant it to those who have hurt us.

How do we go about overcoming the desire to get revenge for that offense that eats away at our souls? How can we get healing for the powerful poison of resentment? The answer is to learn to forgive those who have offended us. We must learn to apply in our lives what we read in the Bible. It is not our beliefs that make us good but, rather, our actions. We will be judged not by what we say but by what we do (see Matthew 25:31–46). Right now, kneel down and repeat this prayer: "Lord, on my own I cannot forgive; grant me Your sweet gift of forgiveness. I need it like the air I breathe." God will answer you immediately. When you arise from your knees, you may not feel any different; but God is faithful to His promises, and softly, tenderly, He will take you through the process. Sometimes it can be painful to forgive others and release the weight of bitterness.

It is possible that our forgiveness will leave the person unchanged. But we are ennobled, and we receive peace. Forgiveness frees us within from tortuous self-accusation, reproach, and desires for vengeance or revenge. Forgiveness quenches the thirst of retaliation. Forgiveness frees us from the chains that enslave the soul and sicken the body. Forgiveness may or may not lead to reconciliation with the other person, but it will eventually produce reconciliation with oneself.

Forgiving does not mean that we resign ourselves powerlessly to those injustices we have suffered or that we approve of such behaviors. Forgiveness does not mean that we stop giving importance to the facts or that we are in agreement with the hurtful position someone has taken against us. It simply means reading the past in a different way, with fresh eyes illuminated by love, healed by the divine eye drops. Forgiveness lifts the burden we have been carrying.

If you have trouble forgiving, do this exercise: Carry a forty-pound sack of potatoes on your back for a week. How does it feel as the days go by? That bag of potatoes, which will begin to rot as the days go by, is like resentment, which is rancid and leaves you crippled. Soon you will be limping along, with that heavy weight throwing you off-balance. The Latin root *rancidus* expresses what I am saying here; it is related to the word *rancor*. It is also related to the Spanish word *rengo*, which means "lame." *Rancidus* expresses two hallmarks of resentment: the condition of something old that has decomposed, that is stale and stagnant, or immobility that prevents advancement. Just like that bag of potatoes that hampers you from moving about with ease, the lack of forgiveness prevents you from living and enjoying your spiritual and emotional life. Get rid of that "sack of potatoes," and you will see how light and enjoyable life is!

But there is still something more that needs to be said regarding forgiveness: we need to learn to bestow it on ourselves.

A study conducted on 213 war veterans showed that those who had difficulty forgiving themselves suffered a higher degree of depression, anxiety, and symptoms of severe post-traumatic stress.[8]

It was January 2014 when I received a phone call from a woman in Salinas, California. She was an administrator at a labor farm where I had ministered to the workers. "Please come and talk with my father, he is very depressed. Twice he has tried to commit suicide." The concerned caller went on to inform me of her father's situation: "Two years ago, at the age of fifty-seven, he left our mother for a much younger woman, but that relationship was short-lived. When he realized what he had done, he returned to our family, but my mother did not take him back. Then he fell into a terrible depression. Finally, my sister and I talked to our mother and asked her to forgive him. My sister and I forgave him before she did because we were greatly worried about his depression. Finally, the whole family forgave him as well. Despite our doing that, his depression has continued. It is clear that he can not forgive himself for his great sin. He had always been a strict Catholic, very rigid and demanding of his family."

I went to see Mr. Guadalupe. I found him with his head down, reclining in a chair in his dim room. I did not know whether he was asleep or meditating. I spoke, but he did not answer. So I decided to apply the same reasoning process he was using on himself:

"You committed a mistake, a great sin," I said.

And then he spoke: "Yes! You are the only one who has told me so. My whole family says that everything is over, but I just can't stop mulling over my sin and suffering the shame of what I did. What happened is something that nobody can change."

"And how much longer do you plan on continuing to punish yourself?" I asked.

The man quickly raised his head and looked me straight in the eye: "I don't know; I haven't given that a thought."

"Well, I'll give you some time, and in a few days we'll talk again."

His answer was as sudden as it was unexpected: "I think it's been enough time. I'm going to stop suffering."

The entire family was happy with his decision. The next day I went to visit him again and share with him the biblical texts that speak of grace and God's forgiveness. My purpose was to fortify him with the Word of God so that he might avoid falling again into depression. He needed to know that his forgiveness was already assured. All he had to do was accept it.

A short time later I received another phone call from the daughter: "My father committed suicide. Can you come to the funeral?"

The third time was the last, I thought. He simply could not forgive himself. Sometimes it is more difficult to forgive yourself than to forgive others. Do not chew on bitterness. Make forgiveness of self and forgiveness of others habitual in your prayer life.

Bible Teaching: Jesus and Forgiveness
(John 8:1–11)

Introduction

Albert Einstein, considered the most brilliant theoretical physicist of the twentieth century, once said, "When the solution is simple, God is answering." That genius had it so right; God does not like complications. He loves simplicity. He wrote His moral law in just Ten Commandments. Although the wisdom contained in those statutes could fill libraries, God synthesized it and thus gave the world the written expression of His love and justice in ten short phrases.

God's law is the expression of His love, the signature of His righteousness.

Why did Jesus save that woman? What did those men accuse her of? What did Jesus write in the dust? Why did He finally say to her, "Go and sin no more"?

In this chapter we spoke of salvation and forgiveness. Have you ever thought about what God should forgive us for? Have you ever thought about why Jesus died? Have you ever thought about what sin really is?

Let's study what the Bible says about God's law:

What is sin according to the Bible? *(1 John 3:4)*

The Bible says that sin is the transgression of the law. But what law is the Bible referring to?

What expression related to the law does the apostle Paul mention? *(Romans 7:7)*

The writer of this Bible passage associates the word *law* with the expression "You shall not covet."

Where else does this expression to "not covet" also appear? *(Exodus 20:17)*

The expression "You shall not covet" is part of the Decalogue, or the Ten Commandments, also known as the moral law.

What else does the Bible tell us about this law? *(Psalm 119:152)*

This testimony, which is the law of God, is as eternal as God.

What similarity exists between the commandments and the character of God? *(Romans 7:12)*
"The law is holy, and the commandment is holy and just and good" (NKJV). God also is holy, just, and good.

Did Jesus want to abolish this law? *(Matthew 5:17)*
Jesus did not come to "destroy" (abolish) but to fulfill the eternal law of God.

What does the law do for us? *(Galatians 3:24)*
The law leads us to Christ, because when we look at ourselves through it and see ourselves as sinners, we feel the need of a Savior.

Conclusion

Jesus saved this woman as an example of His power to save sinners condemned by the law. He wrote in the dust with His finger just as God wrote the law with His finger on Mount Sinai (see Exodus 31:18). And Jesus died and spared us from the condemnation of the law because the law could not be changed. Jesus saves us and transforms us so that we can live in harmony with the spirit of the law of God (see Romans 3:31). One saying goes like this: "The law of God establishes priorities: God first, then people, and things last."

An appeal

Will you accept Jesus' transforming grace to live in harmony with the eternal law of God?

Resolution

I accept the transforming grace of the Lord so that I can live within the spirit of the law.

I sign this in acceptance: _____.

How Much of a Forgiving Person Am I?
Evaluation of Forgiveness

Answer the following ten statements, assigning each a number from 1 to 10, where 1 signifies "Strongly disagree"; 5: "Neither agree nor disagree"; and 10: "Strongly agree."

Statements	Score
1. I will not forgive anyone if they do not apologize and recognize what they have done.	
2. Those who have belittled me and hurt me, even though they don't believe they are at fault, do not deserve my forgiveness.	
3. My inability to forgive is because I remember the past very well.	
4. I cannot forgive because I do not tolerate bad behavior.	
5. My difficulty forgiving makes it hard for me to trust others.	
6. It is difficult to forgive, because it is like downplaying the fault.	
7. Forgiveness is simply felt. It is not a skill.	
8. Since nothing can be done to change things, I tend to keep things to myself and not share my pain with others.	
9. If I forgive, I will be vulnerable; therefore I cannot forgive. I have to protect myself.	
10. I cannot forgive myself for the decisions and mistakes of the past.	

Interpretation for the evaluation of forgiveness

1. Add up the score for each of the ten statements.

2. According to the total sum obtained, consult your results in the following table.

Results table

Score	Interpretation
15 points or fewer	You are an excellent forgiver. Congratulations!
16–29 points	You are quite proficient in the ability to forgive. You have the ability, and you have a positive attitude.
30–49 points	You are moderately competent to forgive. You can improve to become less negative and not remain stuck in the past.

50–69 points	Your ability to forgive is impaired. You have difficulty forgiving, which limits your ability to have a positive attitude and live in the present.
70–84 points	Your ability to forgive is severely damaged. You must work to develop your ability to forgive.
85–100 points	Danger! Your inability to forgive is tremendously affecting your life. Find psychological support and consider attending forgiveness therapy.

1. R. D. Enright and The Human Development Study Group, "Piaget on the Moral Development of Forgiveness: Identity or Reciprocity?" *Human Development* 37, no. 2 (1994): 63–80, doi: 10.1159/00278239.

2. Richard P. Fitzgibbons, "The Cognitive and Emotive Uses of Forgiveness in the Treatment of Anger," *Psychotherapy* 23, no. 4 (1986): 629–633, doi: 10.1037/h0085667.

3. Michael E. McCullough, Everett L. Worthington, and Kenneth C. Rachal, "Interpersonal Forgiving in Close Relationships," *Journal of Personality and Social Psychology* 73, no. 2 (August 1997): 321–336, doi: 10.1037/0022-3514.73.2.321.

4. Frank D. Fincham, Steven R. H. Beach, and Joanne Davila, "Forgiveness and Conflict Resolution in Marriage," *Journal of Family Psychology* 18, no. 1 (March 2004): 72–81, doi: 10.1037/0893-3200.18.1.72.

5. Radhi H. Al-Mabuk, Robert D. Enright, and Paul A. Cardis, "Forgiveness Education With Parentally Love-Deprived Late Adolescents," *Journal of Moral Education* 24, no. 4 (1995): 427–444, doi: 10.1080/0305724950240405.

6. Murray Bradfield and Karl Aquino, "The Effects of Blame Attributions and Offender Likableness on Forgiveness and Revenge in the Workplace," *Journal of Management* 25, no. 5 (October 1999): 607–631, doi: 10.1177/014920639902500501.

7. Kevin S. Seybold et al., "Physiological and Psychological Correlates of Forgiveness," *Journal of Psychology and Christianity* 20, no. 3 (2001): 250–259; McCullough, Worthington, and Rachal, "Interpersonal Forgiving."

8. C. V. O. Witvliet, et al., "Posttraumatic Mental and Physical Health Correlates of Forgiveness and Religious Coping in Military Veterans," *Journal of Traumatic Stress* 17, no. 3 (June 2004): 269–273, doi: 10.1023/B:JOTS.0000029270.47848.e5.

Chapter 3

Joy

Joy and love are the wings to achieve great dreams.
—Johann W. Goethe

Juan Cabrera weighed barely a little more than the crate of tomatoes that he carried on his slight ten-year-old shoulders. What Juan did not know was how the thoughts racing through his mind at that moment would play out in his character and future: *I can't let this crate of tomatoes fall. I can't and I won't. I've got to make it to the end of the street. The lady trusted me with this box of tomatoes, and I mustn't drop it.* After struggling for almost two blocks under that burden, the exhausted boy drew out his last reserve of strength to gently lower the crate off his aching frame. Leaning against a wall to brace himself, he slowly shifted the load onto his thigh and steadied it and then deposited the box down onto the doorstep.

A metaphor for his life.

At ten years old, Juan was learning that no one reaches the top by defeating others; one reaches it by overcoming oneself. He was also aware that everyone has their own hells and their own summits. His hell was his home, and his summit was to earn a few pesos in order to get away from his parents. So here he was, practically living on his own at the age of ten and hauling produce from the village market for customers.

Juan Cabrera was born in Coeneo, Michoacán, Mexico, on a warm afternoon in March 1978. His mother had already given birth to five children and would bear as many more in the next five years. As a child he was pretty much on his own because his mother didn't have time to do much more than make sweet fruit treats to sell from door to door in order to support the family. His father, a very violent man when drunk, spent everything he earned at the bars near where his family lived. Juan was quick to act when his mother gave the warning that his father was about to stagger in late at night. There were

39

knives and potentially dangerous objects to hide, and then he would bundle up the smaller siblings and lead them out like ducklings in a row through the back door of the shack and down the path to his grandmother's house a mile or so away.

By the age of twelve, Juan was a full-fledged street kid. He worked hard, and he was heavily into drugs. He learned to smoke marijuana and drink alcohol, and when he had a few pesos left over, he added cocaine to the mix. That was his life, between drugs and temporary jobs, until he was eighteen years old, when he thought his luck might change. He met Carmen, a scrawny bag of bones that seemed in danger of being blown away by the wind. She had big dark eyes that were affectionate.

The night he met Carmen, Juan had a dream. It was like the vision of the Jewish slave recorded in Psalm 126. The Bible narrates that this poor captive living in Babylonian exile, far from his homeland and suffering nostalgia, dreamed of being released to return home. And then he pleads:

> Lord, change our circumstances for the better,
>   like dry streams in the desert waste!
> Let those who plant with tears
>   reap the harvest with joyful shouts.
> Let those who go out,
>   crying and carrying their seed,
>   come home with joyful shouts,
>   carrying bales of grain! (Psalm 126:4–6, CEB).

Juan dreams that everything changes: he imagines himself returning to his family home, with the same parents, but transformed. He is thrilled to see his brothers and sisters; and Carmen is there too. Carried away with great joy, he cries at being released. His face shines with happiness and he jumps for joy. What an explosion of wonderful emotions sweep over him! He couldn't be happier, until he discovers that it is all a dream. Just like for the Jewish slave.

After that night, Juan came to the realization that the only joy he had known in life was captured in that dream. But if he could dream while asleep, he could also dream while awake. He wanted to give life to his dream and find happiness; so he proposed marriage to Carmen.

After two years of matrimony, Juan and Carmen immigrated to the United States. They crossed the border, but a much more difficult "border" awaited Juan to cross. What Carmen did not know was that Juan was still dependent on drugs to keep him going, to bolster him up in the face of many challenges. Juan's body was paying back the debts he had accumulated since childhood.

He had tried to drown his anguish in alcohol, cigarettes, marijuana, and co-caine, and since arriving in the United States, he had added crystal meth or ice and crack to his list of drugs.

He went to jail three times, not for alcohol or drugs, but for minor inci-dents that any US citizen might have avoided with ease. The problem is that when we are on our way down, it seems that destiny pushes us even further into the abyss. Every time Juan got out of jail, he was deported. After the last deportation, when he again crossed the border into the United States, Carmen had already decided to leave him. She wanted to protect their only son, Eden, from the wayward example of his father.

Events in Juan's life were now rapidly coming to a head. It seemed like he was being carried forward by an overpowering wind toward the crossroads of his destiny. He could sense it. Juan knew that he had to change, but he didn't know how. During that week when he returned from Mexico, Carmen's mother had a conversation with her daughter: "Juan is not a bad person. He is a good man, just confused. Give him one last chance."

That same afternoon, Adventist pastor Pedro Rascón phoned Carmen to pray for her and Juan. As they talked, the pastor also urged her, "Give your husband one more chance." The following day, Juan had a hearing before the judge. He had been granted an extension prior to deportation; the judge knew Juan would cross the border once again, but with mercy and wisdom the magistrate was giving him the option to definitively cross an internal border toward happiness. He said to him: "I've erased your record, because I do not want you to appear before me again. Take advantage of this opportunity."

Juan received those words of grace as though from on high; and at the age of twenty-seven, he abandoned drugs and gave himself to Christ.

My wife, Florencia, and I are seated in the dining room at Juan and Car-men's house as I write these lines. They are in front of us with their children: Eden, fourteen, and Alonso, seven. Juan has built every piece of furniture decorating their home. He is a determined and responsible person, like the boy who carried the box of tomatoes at the beginning of this story. He takes great care with everything that comes from his prodigious hands. Carmen has turned their house into a peaceful home.

"Who do you have to thank for this?" I ask Juan.

"My mother-in-law, Celia Vargas," he responds, "for her unconditional love. And pastors Pedro Rascón and Edwin López for visiting me in jail and showing me a new path. And Jesus, my Lord. I feel deep joy in my heart. I carry my past inside me; I cannot forget it, but I decide what I want to hold onto from that past. I choose that dream I had when I was young; I choose to think that God led me and freed me in order to give me such great happiness."

Juan was born again, and his joy is the gift of the Holy Spirit to those who give their lives to Christ: "The fruit of the Spirit is love, *joy*, peace, patience, kindness, goodness, faith" (Galatians 5:22, WEB, emphasis added).

Juan's joy rested on the fact that he was born again. The judge gave him that last chance to finally cross the border into a new life, but only Jesus could give him new life.

What does science say about joy?

A large body of literature confirms the relationship between happiness and good health. For example, a study of 36,598 people who were followed for more than five years found that those who were happier within the study group had 26 percent less risk of dying prematurely from stress-related diseases and coronary dysfunctions.[1] This is due to the fact that positive emotions affect biological processes, improving the functioning of the immune system and increasing antibody levels or cell defenses.[2]

Certainly the most important research on happiness and longevity that has been done so far was the study of 180 nuns who had kept diaries with biographical data in their adolescence. A differentiation was established between the most cheerful and those who exhibited little cheerfulness. They were followed for seventy years, and it was found that a large majority (90 percent) of the most cheerful were still alive at eighty-five, but only 34 percent of the less cheerful remained alive. In a follow-up it was found that 54 percent of the cheerful ones were still alive at ninety-four years, while only 11 percent of the less cheerful still survived. Those differences speak for themselves concerning the benefits of joy.[3]

For many years it has been known that laughter is great for one's health. Perhaps the most striking case that led science to recognize the wholesome effects of laughter was that of Norman Cousins, who suffered an illness diagnosed as ankylosing spondylitis, a rare progressive paralysis that attacks the legs, neck, and back and produces fever and severe pain throughout the body. Specialists gave Norman little hope of life: only one patient out of five hundred had been saved. Cousins reasoned that if negative emotions sicken a person, then positive emotions should offer a cure.

He shut himself away for several months in a hotel and dedicated himself to resting, watching comedies, and reading humorous books. In effect, he was "self-medicating" on laughter: "It worked. I made the joyous discovery that ten minutes of genuine belly laughter had an anesthetic effect and would give me at least two hours of pain-free sleep. When the pain-killing effect of the laughter wore off, we would switch on the motion-picture projector again, and, not infrequently, it would lead to another pain-free sleep interval."[4] And this is how he recovered fully.

Jesus and joy

Now he was teaching in one of the synagogues on the Sabbath, and a woman was there who had been disabled . . . for eighteen years. She was bent over and could not straighten herself up completely. When Jesus saw her, he called her to him and said, "Woman, you are freed from your infirmity." Then he placed his hands on her, and immediately she straightened up and praised God. But the president of the synagogue, indignant because Jesus had healed on the Sabbath, said to the crowd, "There are six days on which work should be done! So come and be healed on those days, and not on the Sabbath day." Then the Lord answered him, "You hypocrites! Does not each of you on the Sabbath untie his ox or his donkey from its stall, and lead it to water? Then shouldn't this woman, a daughter of Abraham whom Satan bound for eighteen long years, be released from this imprisonment on the Sabbath day?" When he said this all his adversaries were humiliated, but the entire crowd was rejoicing at all the wonderful things he was doing (Luke 13:10–17, NET).

Who was this woman discovered by Jesus in the synagogue that Sabbath? We have almost no information about her, we don't know whether she was married, whether she had children, what her appearance was like, who her friends were, or how she behaved, and neither do we know her name. The biblical text leaves us in total darkness regarding her life story. The single significant fact is that for eighteen years she had suffered with her illness. She was a woman with a chronic disability, long condemned to a life of solitude. Subjected to subhuman conditions, she lived in a shameful and humiliating situation without being able to establish easy eye contact with another adult.

How old was she when the disease struck? It seems unlikely that she could have been more than thirty years old, since the deterioration would have left her unable to even hobble to the synagogue. Perhaps she was younger when this affliction came upon her and began deforming her spine. I wonder whether she had been married and whether her husband had abandoned his disabled wife. There is no mention of anyone accompanying her there at the worship place. We can surmise that she was a woman condemned to loneliness and abandonment.

How did she endure for eighteen years that torture of solitude? Perhaps at first she held on to the illusion of finding healing through the medical professionals of those times. Gradually, her physical discomfort grew beyond all that anyone should ever have to bear in life. Disappointment after disappointment came in her quest for a cure, only to realize at last that there was no human remedy for her situation. Anxiety led to frustration, and that finally led to total helplessness. To venture outside was to expose herself to the people's morbid curiosity or pity.

What to do? Well, seek the help of God. This seemed to be her last and only hope. And where could she possibly find Him? In the synagogue, of course, the place where religion was taught and the power of God was supposed to be revealed. So for years the only time she ventured out of her house was to go to the synagogue, with the intimate desire to find salvation for her body and soul.

But what did this suffering soul find in that special place meant for salvation? There were only religious leaders dulled by a rigorous and compulsive orthodoxy, dominated by the imperatives of duty, which incapacitated them to see the joy of health. They were also "hunchbacks," living a life bent over by the weight of obligations. They only knew of rituals and strict adherence to the rules. They lived under the mandates of "dos" and "don'ts." The only things they understood were rigidity and the hardness of the statutes and rules. More than custodians of the law, they were subjects to duty and victims to formalism. Then, in stepped Jesus with a clear demonstration of God's sovereignty and true religion. The Great Healer gave a lesson on freedom and joy. A crippled daughter of heaven received at last the healing touch she had longed for. Jesus healed the woman and surely produced the greatest expression of joy in a synagogue on the Sabbath.

The message of freedom and joy was not given just for the woman healed that day or for those who attended that synagogue long ago; it was given for all those who through faith in Christ are invited to live the experience of a new life, and among these is Juan Cabrera.

When her miracle took place, that woman spontaneously burst with joy and praise for what Jesus did in her behalf. I imagine her dancing and laughing like crazy. She laughed with her mouth, and her eyes sparkled with happy tears; in her body and soul she praised God. I imagine that this woman continued laughing for the rest of her life. She felt that laughter welling up in contentment while strengthening her against all manner of external demands. Physically, mentally, and spiritually she must have lived a very good life thereafter.

Laughter is the sunshine of the soul, the light of its existence. It noticeably improves the quantity and quality of life. Paul expresses it this way: "Now godliness combined with contentment brings great profit. For we have brought nothing into this world, and so we cannot take a single thing out either. But if we have food and shelter, we will be satisfied with that" (1 Timothy 6:6–8, NET).

That healed woman, Juan Cabrera, and all those who have decided to place their burdens on Jesus will live this kind of joy that comes only from God.

Why and how to defend joy

The crippled woman was born again after the intervention of Jesus. She was born in two ways: to a new existence in this world and in the hope of eternal life. We said before that true joy is second in the fruit of the Holy Spirit (Galatians 5:22), and it is the expression of the new birth. The Holy Spirit gives joy because He gives life.

In chapter three of John, Jesus explains, in dialogue with a teacher of Israel, the process of new birth through the Holy Spirit:

> Now a certain man, a Pharisee named Nicodemus, who was a member of the Jewish ruling council, came to Jesus at night and said to him, "Rabbi, we know that you are a teacher who has come from God. For no one could perform the miraculous signs that you do unless God is with him." Jesus replied, "I tell you the solemn truth, unless a person is born from above, he cannot see the kingdom of God." Nicodemus said to him, "How can a man be born when he is old? He cannot enter his mother's womb and be born a second time, can he?"
>
> Jesus answered, "I tell you the solemn truth, unless a person is born of water and spirit, he cannot enter the kingdom of God. What is born of the flesh is flesh, and what is born of the Spirit is spirit. Do not be amazed that I said to you, 'You must all be born from above.' . . ."
>
> Nicodemus replied, "How can these things be?" Jesus answered, . . . "No one has ascended into heaven except the one who descended from heaven—the Son of Man. Just as Moses lifted up the serpent in the wilderness, so must the Son of Man be lifted up, so that everyone who believes in him may have eternal life" (John 3:1–9, 13–15, NET).

This text expresses two great truths about the new birth: In the first place, it helps us to realize that new birth does not depend on us any more than does normal birth in this world. And secondly, we learn that we need to accept the One who came down from heaven to be lifted up on the cross. Life comes from God and salvation, from His Son. To receive this in the heart is to be born again, and that is the only thing that will give us true joy in this life.

Christ is the joy of the believer. We read in Philippians 4:4, "Always be full of joy in the Lord" (NLT). His Person is our joy. In His presence we find "fullness of joy" (Psalm 16:11, MEV). Jesus said, "These things I have spoken to you, that my joy may be in you, and that your joy may be full" (John 15:11, ESV). The joy of the believer is a state of inner enrichment; it promotes a feeling of satisfaction with what one has because the believer feels accepted by God as well as redeemed and guided by Him.

Jesus said that joy can arise even out of sadness and pain. He illustrated that by the example of a mother giving birth. Those words were spoken at the time that He announced His approaching death and departure from the world. The disciples were saddened by the thought of the coming separation. For three years they had practically lived with the Master, and now He was going to leave them. They suffered with this awareness. But then Jesus encouraged them with the hope that He would return for the second time, never to be separated again from them and all those who believe in Him (John 14:1–3). That "blessed hope" (Titus 2:13) has been at the heart of the Christian faith throughout the centuries and millennia. Additionally, and for the duration, He promised them the companionship of the Holy Spirit. This Divine Person would give the disciples of that time, and of all time, the blessed permanent presence of Christ in their lives. That experience would be like a rebirth, a new birth of faith and joy, to dispel the shadows of anguish.

For this reason, anchored in this hope, turn your heart over to Jesus again today. Make this your practice every day, and it will fortify your emotional vitality, invigorate your enthusiasm, and liven your hope and commitment.

The eight secrets of joy

Following are eight secrets to a joyful life that you can begin to implement in your daily life:

- Accept Christ.
- Cultivate optimism: Learn that no matter what happens or how bad things may seem today, life goes on, and tomorrow will be better.
- Nurture friendships, for this will give you joy. In doing this, you will be remembered, because people eventually forget what you said, maybe even what you did, but they will never forget how you made them feel.
- Attend a church and live your faith in community.
- Guard your health: Rest and nourish yourself in a healthy way. Breathe fresh air every morning. Drink plenty of water each day.
- Get physical exercise.
- Always help others. Delight in showing kindness to the needy.

Bible Teaching: Jesus and Joy
(Luke 13:10–17)

Introduction

A young woman sold fruit at her stand in the market, and every Saturday she closed shop because of her Sabbath-keeping belief. One of the regular customers thought it was foolish of her to do that. He argued that every day is equal before God, but she defended her doctrine. One day the man came by and again wanted to make his point. The young woman was busy serving others, so he simply lined up seven grapefruits and, catching her attention, pointed out that they were all alike. Cleverly, the young woman snatched the last grapefruit and placed a juicy orange in its place. The man caught on without the need for many words: the seventh day is sweeter than the others.

The biblical account says that Jesus went to the synagogue to teach the Word of God on a Sabbath day. In an earlier chapter of Luke we read that it was His "custom" to go to the synagogue on the Sabbath, for it was the house of God (4:16). On one of those Sabbaths, Jesus healed a woman who had been afflicted for eighteen years. According to the passage, some were angry with Him for working a miracle in her behalf. Why were they angry? Did Jesus disobey the law of God when He healed the woman on the Sabbath? How does the Sabbath relate to joy, happiness, and peace?

In the previous study we saw the role of the eternal law of God and the transforming power of Christ that gives us the capacity to live in harmony with the spirit of the law. That law is the basis of His government.

Let's review what the Bible says about the Sabbath:

How does the Sabbath relate to the eternal law expressed in the Ten Commandments? *(Exodus 20:8–11)*

The fourth commandment of the Decalogue commands us to observe the Sabbath, the seventh day of the week, as the day of worship.

Was the observance of this commandment exclusively for the Jews? *(Genesis 2:1–3)*

When God finished with the creation of the earth and of Adam and Eve, the first thing He did was set aside the Sabbath day, the seventh day of the week, as a day of worship, so that all creation recently created by His hand might worship Him before anything else.

What did Jesus say about the Sabbath? *(Mark 2:27)*
Jesus reaffirmed the idea that the Sabbath was not only for the Jews but for all humanity.

What is the relationship between Jesus and the Sabbath? *(Mark 2:28)*
As Lord of the Sabbath, Jesus gives meaning to the commandment. Since it is impossible to keep the Sabbath without a connection to Him, whoever pretends to obey without the grace of Christ misses the way. Jesus said He is the One who gives us true rest (Matthew 11:28).

How should we keep the Sabbath? *(Isaiah 58:13, 14)*
When we live by a faith that transforms, we delight in doing God's will. Therefore, we observe the Sabbath as a result of receiving grace and being transformed by it.

For how long will the seventh-day Sabbath be kept as a day of worship? *(Isaiah 66:22, 23)*
Since the Sabbath is part of the eternal law of God, its observance will remain for eternity. Since Jesus did not change the law, but confirmed it, His followers also are to obey this commandment (Acts 16:13).

What is the relationship between the Sabbath and joy? *(Hebrews 4:8–10)*
When we understand that we can live under the grace of God, which does not invalidate the law, by the power of that grace we rest in God. As a result, we live the joy of salvation (Psalm 51:12).

Conclusion
The healing of the woman on the Sabbath is a symbol of the liberation we experience when we observe that day with Jesus. Thus, He reaffirmed the commandment that brings joy and happiness to our lives when we connect with Jesus. It is said that "the Sabbath is the birthday of the world."

An appeal
Will you accept rest in Jesus, which brings joy and happiness to life, by observing this commandment?

My resolve

I accept this rest in Jesus; I accept His grace that enables me to observe the Sabbath.

I sign this in acceptance: _____.

How Cheerful Am I?
Assessing My Level of Joy

For each of the following phrases or questions, mark the point on the scale that you think best describes you.

1. Overall, I would say I am . . .

Not happy						Very happy
1	2	3	4	5	6	7

2. Compared with my friends or peers, I think I am . . .

Not happy						Very happy
1	2	3	4	5	6	7

3. Some people generally are very happy: they enjoy life despite what happens; they take full advantage of life. To what extent does this characterize you?

Not happy						Very happy
1	2	3	4	5	6	7

4. Some people, in general, do not seem to be happy, even though they are not depressed. To what extent does this apply to you?

Not happy						Very happy
1	2	3	4	5	6	7

Interpretation for assessing my level of joy

1. The score for questions 1, 2, and 3 is the same as the number where you put your mark.

2. For question 4, it is the opposite. If the answer is 1, then it is 7 points; 2 = 6; 3 = 5; 4 = 4; 5 = 3; 6 = 2; and 7 = 1.

3. Add the results of the four questions. The interpretation of the score follows.

Results

24 to 28 points .... very happy

19 to 23 points .... happy

14 to 18 points .... average

8 to 13 points .... unhappy

4 to 7 points .... very unhappy

---

1. Julia Boehm et al., "A Prospective Study of Positive Psychological Well-Being and Coronary Heart Disease," *Health Psychology* 30, no. 3 (May 2011): 259–267, doi: 10.1037 /a0023124.

2. Carlos D. Tajer, "Alegría del corazón: Emociones positivas y salud cardiovascular," *Revista Argentina de Cardiología* 80, no. 4 (2012): 325–332.

3. Danner, Snowdon, and Friesen, "Positive Emotions in Early Life and Longevity" (see chap. 1, n. 7).

4. Norman Cousins and Rene Dubos, *Anatomy of an Illness as Perceived by the Patient* (New York: Norton, 2001), 43.

Chapter 4

Generosity

Command them to do good, to be rich in good deeds,
and to be generous and willing to share.
—1 Timothy 6:18, NIV

Since childhood I have always realized that there is special beauty in a woman, no matter the years she might have seen. What comes to mind when I remember Ofelia is that a woman can be very beautiful even if she has little outward attractiveness. That is how it was in the case of Ofelia. When I was eight, she was about thirty. She was thin, bony, and figureless, with wrinkles on her face, and her exaggeratedly hooked nose culminated in a sort of wartlike mole. All in all, I thought she was quite ugly. Ofelia never had a boyfriend, nor had she ever received a kiss of romantic affection. In addition, the boys said that she wasn't all there when it came to being smart. That is to say that her IQ was below the average of the population of the neighborhood.

Every week I saw her pass by in front of my house. She paused a few seconds to greet me and ask how I was even though I was a child or precisely because I was a child. Sometimes she would mention that she was going to the hospital to see her doctor. Later I learned that, in fact, she was going to a psychologist for counseling. I think that life must not have been easy for Ofelia. However, today, after more than fifty years, I remember her not so much for her physical appearance but for her big, warm heart.

Ofelia loved children. It was something I did not see often in "normal" people or in good-looking, intelligent people. For me, that made Ofelia different but in an endearing way. Generous and kindhearted, she had a commendable habit: twice a week she visited the nearby orphanage and spent time with the children. She would take one or another out for a walk. She seemed to me like the best version of a mother (I say "the best" because there are mothers who mistreat their children or are harsh with them). Despite being single, she had gotten official approval to take a child under her care several afternoons per week. Usually, she took the child to the zoo, the park, a place of amusement, or the movies. They would get something tasty to eat, and together they would enjoy a great afternoon of fun. All the orphanage children looked forward to Ofelia's visits and an invitation out; and to be sure, for her, those outings were the most important moments of her life.

Sometimes she would tell me with enthusiasm about her delightful times with these orphaned children who so much needed love. Ofelia was that loving heart for many of those children. When she spoke, her face lit up with a kind and sympathetic expression to the point that her appearance was transformed, becoming pleasant and even attractive. I'm certain those loving deeds improved Ofelia's health and gave meaning to her life. One thing I learned from her was that if you want to know a person, do not stop at just their outward appearance or beliefs; don't just listen to their words, but observe their behavior.

"Without goodness there cannot be happiness," said Thomas Carlyle. Kindness gives life to dreams.

What does science say about generosity?

It is said that kindness is the most acute form of intelligence. We now know conclusively, through abundant empirical evidence, that generosity is a virtue beneficial to others and to oneself; it is a source of happiness. A group of people was asked to do five acts of service per week for six weeks. Each Sunday evening the participants got together to report on the various deeds they had done, which went something like this: "I donated blood," "I visited a nursing home," "I gave money to a man who lived on the street," "I thanked my professor for his interesting class presentations," and so on. Upon completion of the study, the results were eye-opening. It was found that participants who served or complimented others experienced a significant increase in their own personal happiness. They commented on how much more beneficial and useful they felt; their self-esteem rose through showing kindness and appreciation to others; they simply felt better, while their general sensations of guilt, discomfort, or suffering seemed to decrease.

It was also observed that performing actions on behalf of others often triggered a cascade of positive social consequences because the recipients of kindness were motivated within to respond in like manner. Many people are appreciative and thankful for what they receive and will reciprocate with generosity or do thoughtful deeds to reward the kindness shown to them.[1]

Other studies have shown that those who spent part of their time helping others afflicted with the same disease felt noticeably better while improving their rate of survival.[2]

Several European governments funded research to see whether volunteering was favorable to health. Emphasis was given to studies where volunteers faced a heightened level of risk to their own health, especially in hospital service. For example, the government of the Netherlands studied nearly four thousand people sixteen years old or older performing volunteer work, focusing on the subjective contentment levels of the participants. The results confirmed that the volunteers exhibited higher levels of happiness than people who did not volunteer when that activity did not exceed five hours per week. When the time commitment was increased, decreased levels of happiness were noted along with an increase of stress.[3] The conclusion: helping others can be a very positive factor in promoting one's own happiness.

Jesus and generosity

Despite the passage of centuries, the phrase of Augustine of Hippo still holds true: "I sought God and could not find Him, then I sought my brother and finally we three met."

Jesus was the Master of generosity. He practiced the deepest form of giving; He didn't just give things, He gave of Himself. During His ministry He poured out gifts and kindness on foreigners, the sick, children, and women and even on His enemies. His whole life was a commitment to humanity, until the day of His death when He gave everything.

The love manifested in Jesus came from the Father, the God of all giving. He gave His Son the mission of giving Himself to humanity. That is why Jesus said, "All things have been handed over to me by my Father, and no one knows the Son except the Father, and no one knows the Father except the Son and anyone to whom the Son chooses to reveal him" (Matthew 11:27, ESV). When we know Jesus, we know the Father. And the joy of giving is the revelation of the Son in your heart.

Philip, one of Jesus' followers, received this revelation and learned from Him how to use the gift of generosity in benefit to others. The Gospels describe this disciple as sociable, interested in others; he could not stop sharing his experiences with friends. For him, people were of great importance; he was more interested in human beings than in things.

There is a story in the Gospel of John that portrays Philip just as he was: the episode where he first meets Jesus and is completely fascinated (see John 1:43–46). Philip was not an intellectual, a theorist, or an individual concerned about theological or philosophical abstractions; he was a practical man. After hearing the Nazarene, he was convinced that He was the Messenger of

Heaven, the Son of God. And when Jesus said, "Follow Me," he followed.

Philip was so excited about his discovery that he could not help but run right out and tell everyone that he had found the Son of God. The first friend he wanted to tell was Nathanael, a studious young man, thoughtful, and rather quiet and observant. Only, in his enthusiasm to tell about finding the Messiah, Philip made the mistake of mentioning where Jesus hailed from: "We have found him, of whom Moses in the law, and the prophets, wrote: Jesus of Nazareth, the son of Joseph," (verse 45, WEB). Nathanael picked up immediately that here was a fact that did not fit the prophetic narrative. How could He come from Nazareth? What prophecy says that the Messiah would come from there? He could not come from that northern part of the country because that region was always subject to foreign invasions and most of the population was of mixed blood. Families in that region wouldn't retain a pure Jewish heritage, he reasoned.

Faced with this objection, Philip simply said, "Come and see" (verse 46). For Philip the human experience was more important than the subtleties of reasoning and prejudices of culture. Living realities and personal exchange are what define a person, not theory. Indeed, the name *Philip* captures this concept: it comes from the Greek, *Philos-hipos*, which means, "a friend of horses." The man was such a friend to fellow humans that who could doubt that he had a soft spot in his heart for animals as well?

The Master knew His disciple, so He appealed to him when He needed someone to help feed a crowd: "Where shall we buy bread for these people to eat?" (John 6:5, NIV). When asked this question by Jesus, Philip made a rapid calculation and answered, "Two hundred denarii worth of bread would not be enough for each of them to get a little" (verse 7, ESV). Surely he would like to have had that money to buy bread for all those people, but it was far more than the disciples had. On that occasion, Jesus honored Philip's sensitivity by multiplying the loaves and the fish. A generous heart finds extraordinary ways even with very little to "feed the hungry."

Why and how to practice generosity?

The only statement of Jesus on generosity outside of the Gospels is found in the book of Acts, written by the disciple Luke. It reads: "In all things I gave you an example, that so laboring you ought to help the weak, and to remember the words of the Lord Jesus, that he himself said, 'It is more blessed to give than to receive' " (Acts 20:35, WEB).

What did the Master of Nazareth mean when He said that the one who gives is happier than the one who receives?

Giving can sometimes pose dangers: Just try helping someone regularly for a time, and then, when you cease to do so, you might find yourself now considered that person's worst enemy. And we know that lending money to some folks means you will likely never see them again. Giving can also be less than altruistic, as when the giver has ulterior or self-serving motives. Popular wisdom says: "When the alms are high, even saints grow nervous."

So, then, what is the meaning of Jesus' declaration?

Every human relationship involves giving and taking. He who gives receives, and he who receives gives. But this balance is not without effort and struggle. Not many days ago, a woman said to me, "I'm tired of giving and never receiving anything from my husband." But it is possible that the husband simply could not give her what she was asking for. Maybe he was worried about getting further into debt and was unable to come up with cash for what his wife requested. The couple really needed to sit down together and consider their finances and what was or was not at that moment within their means. There needs to be an understanding balance between giving and receiving. Without this balance, relationships can die.

It seems that we cannot give without expecting something in return or receive without feeling obligated to give. Yesterday, while writing this chapter, I asked my wife what was easier for her—to give or to receive.

"It depends," she said. "But I think that sometimes it is more difficult to receive than to give."

"Why?" I asked.

"It's not easy to receive a gift. Because to accept something I do not really deserve burdens me with a feeling of duty to reciprocate, with a certain sense of guilt."

This idea of an eye for an eye and a tooth for tooth seems to be deeply engrained in us. Apparently, it applies not just in matters of justice but also in matters of the heart. If I receive, then I must give.

However, I know many people who only like to receive. They give nothing, or when they give something, they give it very sparingly; because that is the way it is in their meager lives. These selfish people live small lives, even though they may have lots of money. I had a very rich aunt who lived as though she was miserably poor. She wouldn't even buy a washing machine but instead spent long hours a day washing by hand, "in order to save money." And what exactly was she saving? Nothing! On the contrary, she was wasting her time. But mental scarcity is not an act, it is an attitude.

Some, on the other hand, do not like to receive anything, because they do not want to give in return. They run from any relationship that opens them up to a wider world and might jeopardize the safety of their tight little universe. There are marriages that live only for themselves, not even for their children. They give only to themselves. Nothing opens us up to the world and promotes self-denial quite like having a child, but there are couples that are devoid of selflessness. They do not open their hearts to the world; they are consumed in their own selfishness. They are like the fig tree Jesus cursed for not bearing fruit (see Matthew 21:19).

My mother-in-law, Olga, was a very generous woman. Not long ago, a cousin of my wife commented to her that as a child she remembered her parents saying that Olga was the one who had married the best among the sisters, because she always was able to give good gifts. But it wasn't because my mother-in-law was wealthier than her sisters, like the cousin insinuated. It was because Olga lived in abundance of spirit. She was a generous soul. In her home there was plenty of food for everyone. And because she gave from her heart so liberally people assumed she was well off. Olga bestowed that gift of giving on my wife (and I must confess that sometimes it worries me how much she likes to give gifts).

There are poor folks who seem rich and rich folks living as though they are poor. It is not a question of quantity but of human quality. On one occasion, Jesus watched certain wealthy people pouring their offerings into the temple collection box, and then along came a widow with only two mites, which together equaled a quadrant, the smallest of the Roman coins. Then, "he called unto him his disciples and saith to them, Verily I say unto you, That this poor widow hath cast more in, than all they which have cast into the treasury; For all they did cast in of their abundance; but she of her want did cast in all she had, even all her living" (Mark 12:43, 44, KJV). That widow was very poor, but Jesus did not say, "Keep the money because you are poor"; instead, He praised her generous spirit. On another occasion a woman anointed His feet with "very expensive perfume" (Matthew 26:7, NIV). He chided certain disciples for criticizing her act. Jesus did not refuse that expensive gift, because it was necessary for that woman's grateful heart to express itself far beyond common limits.

But what is the deeper meaning of "it is more blessed to give than to receive"?

Jesus was not saying that he who gives is happier because he gets the upper hand or because he has put the receiver in a position of having to reciprocate in kind. Neither does He say that it is easier to give than to receive. Jesus says that he who gives is more blessed or, rather, happier.

It is not easy to give. It takes effort to give; you have to water the plant of love with perseverance. It is more natural for human beings to receive than to give. Bestowing openly on another does not come naturally. If you don't think that's so, just take a look around you. We live surrounded by separate and secluded islands. Everyone is looking at their own belly buttons. This is a country famous for its communication technology but filled with solitary, isolated souls. In each breast there is a heart hungering for love, affection, and recognition.

Jesus' declaration has three major consequences for the spirit:

Giving confronts us with our own identity. What are we? Why are we in this world? What are the fruits of my life? Jesus' statement makes me wonder whether I have fruits to give and what kind of tree I am. It urges us to think about this because we cannot give what we do not have. Jesus said with respect to not bearing fruit: "Whoever has, to him more will be given; but whoever does not have, even what he has will be taken away from him" (Mark 4:25, NKJV). This means that no matter how little or how much we have, death will eventually take it all away. "What will a man give in exchange for his soul?" (Matthew 16:26, NKJV). If he is dead to life, his waters do not flow, just like the stagnant waters of a swamp.

A modern German tale relates that a rich man died and went to his reward. He knocked on the door, and an angel greeted him, asking what he wanted. The rich man said, "I want a room with a view of Earth, great food, and Internet connection."

The angel, not very willing, granted him the three requests and said, "Enjoy; I will return in a thousand years." A thousand years later, the angel returned, looked through the peephole, and saw the rich gentleman looking bored. When he opened the door, the man blurted out, "Is this heaven? It's horrible."

"No," answered the angel. "You're wrong. This is hell."

Giving frees us from ourselves. It is a call to freedom. It lifts us out of our old comfort zones and safety nets. We are slaves of things. Giving is the best exercise to feeling the fresh air of freedom, which infuses peace and joy in the heart. Zacchaeus felt this freedom—the rich tax collector, hated by the Jews and despised by the Romans. When he was born again, he said, "Behold, Lord, the half of my goods I give to the poor; and if I have defrauded any one of anything, I restore it fourfold" (Luke 19:8, RSV). To give becomes a part of our spiritual nature received from Christ when we are born again. Being born again, we receive the nature of God, who is love, and the Holy Spirit enables us to give with love and generosity.

To give launches us into the cycle of life and shows us the way in which we should walk. It makes us part of the purpose of creation. Nature is a symphony of giving. The sun gives its heat and light, air gives us oxygen to breathe, water sustains all life on earth, and from the ground come forth fruits. This is the love of the Creator.

Jesus was radical in this matter: He told the rich young man to sell every-thing and give it to the poor (see Matthew 19:21). But, I confess, if I propose this to my wife, she will toss me out of the house, even though she loves to give wonderful gifts. Perhaps it would be impossible to sell everything I have and give to the poor. It would simply add another poor person to this world, and I would have to become a beggar. It is just as impossible to do that as it is to forgive "seventy times seven" (Matthew 18:21, 22, MEV). If my neigh-bor crashes into my car 490 times, and I forgive him, long before getting to that magic number there will be no car left! When Jesus said "go and sell," and "forgive seventy times seven," He showed us a horizon to keep in sight. The geographical horizon orients us regarding location, but we never actually "arrive" because it is always that much further beyond us. But if we ignore the contours of the horizon, we can become disoriented. On a moonless night, there is no horizon to see. The morning sun brings it back into view. Christ is the sun that illuminates our spiritual horizon.

When we give, we adopt the character of Christ, who gave His all for you and me. To give thoughtfully and generously gives life to your dreams.

Bible Teaching: Jesus and Generosity
(John 1:43–46)

Introduction

On one occasion, the philosopher and writer Aldous Huxley said to one of his assistants, "I suppose you will go to church. Why not stay home and talk with me about religion?"

"Oh," replied his assistant, "I'm not capacitated enough to answer your questions and arguments."

But Huxley continued: "What I want is for you to tell me what your religion did for you."

Throughout the entire morning, the Christian related what he had experienced in his faith. Then Huxley said, "I'd give my right arm to believe like that."

What happened with Philip, who responded so quickly to the invitation of Jesus?

How does this text demonstrate the power of God's grace to produce in us a different life?

In the previous study we spoke about resting in God and that His peace is the fruit of a changed life.

Let's consider what the Bible says about a faith that works:

How can we live the experience of faith? *(Romans 10:17)*

Having direct contact with the Bible (God's Written Word) produces in us a life of faith and profound changes in behavior.

What benefits come to us when we live by faith? *(Habakkuk 2:4; Romans 5:1)*

By faith we achieve righteousness, and justified by faith we have peace with God.

What is faith? *(Hebrews 11:1)*

Faith is believing what is not seen but also confidence in the person we know and love. A child climbs a ladder confidently if he knows that his father, whom he loves and trusts, will extend his arms to catch him if he falls.

What benefits come from knowing God? *(John 17:3)*

When we are justified by God through faith in Christ, eternity opens before us. The Bible says: "And this is life eternal, that they might know thee" (KJV); knowing Jesus makes us righteous and gives us eternal life.

How I can know God? *(John 14:7–9)*

To know Jesus is to know God because Jesus came to show us what God is like.

How can I know Jesus? *(John 5:39)*

Jesus is the central character in the Bible, and to know Him you have to meditate on His Word. We should read Scripture daily to know Jesus better.

How is true faith expressed? Is there a relationship between Philip's faith and his concern for the needy? *(James 2:14–26; 1 Thessalonians 1:3)*

Because Jesus knew Philip's heart, He appealed to him when he needed someone to help feed the crowd (John 6:5). Philip's faith was expressed in his vocation of helping others. True faith is always manifested by "the works of love."

Conclusion

When Philip met Jesus, faith was born in him that enabled him to live a transformed and generous life. After experiencing faith in Jesus, he told his friend: "Come and see"; that is, try it for yourself. When you try Jesus out for yourself, you will begin to live a life of faith and transformation (2 Corinthians 3:18). Augustine said, "Faith is to believe what you do not see, and the reward of this faith is to see what you believe."

An appeal

Will you accept the invitation of God to look for Him in Scripture every day in order to live a life of constant transformation?

My resolve

I accept the grace of God in Christ that enables me to draw closer to Him through His Word.

I sign this in acceptance: _____.

How Generous Am I?
Assessment of My Generosity

Questions	Yes	Maybe	No
1. Do you give money to those who ask for alms?			
2. Would you work as a volunteer in a nongovernmental organization (NGO)?			
3. If a neighbor's car will not start, would you offer to drive them to work?			
4. Are you tolerant of noisy children on your street without complaining?			
5. Would you give up your seat for someone else?			
6. Are you kind to animals?			
7. Do you think that crimes should be punished less severely?			
8. Would you offer to volunteer for visits to a hospital?			
9. Would you help carry someone's groceries out to their car in the parking lot?			
10. If your neighbor is sick, would you do their shopping?			
11. Do you give money to charity?			
12. After a traffic accident, would you offer to take someone home?			
13. Do you show compassion for those who are underprivileged?			
14. If you saw a child crying, would you try to discover the reason?			
15. If your friend is short on money, would you lend him some?			
16. Would you help someone who is lost?			
17. Are you always friendly to sick people?			
18. Would you help an old person cross the street?			
19. Would you help a neighbor fix his fence?			
20. Do you open your home to others?			

Interpretation for the assessment of my generosity

1. You can obtain the score for each question by assigning the yes column 2 points; the maybe column 1 point; and the no column 0 points.

2. Add the scores for all twenty questions.

3. The interpretation of your total score follows:

Results

35 to 40 points .... Very generous. Excellent!

25 to 34 points .... Generous. Very good.

15 to 24 points .... A bit generous. You can improve.

5 to 14 points .... Not very generous. You need to learn generosity.

0 to 4 points .... Not generous at all. You need to be generous.

---

1. Sonja Lyubomirsky, *The How of Happiness: A Scientific Approach to Getting the Life You Want* (New York, Penguin Press, 2007), 94.

2. Carolyn E. Schwartz and Rabbi Meir Sendor, "Helping Others Helps Oneself: Response Shift Effects in Peer Support," *Social Science and Medicine* 48, no. 11 (June 1999): 1563–1575, doi: 10.1016/S0277-9536(99)00049-0.

3. Cretien Van Campen, Alice H. de Boer, and Jurjen Iedema, "Are Informal Caregivers Less Happy Than Noncaregivers? Happiness and the Intensity of Caregiving in Combination With Paid and Voluntary Work," *Scandinavian Journal of Caring Sciences* 27, no. 1 (March 2013): 44–50, doi: 10.1111/j.1471-6712.2012.00998.x.

Chapter 5

Health

Health is not everything, but without health, everything is nothing.
—Arthur Schopenhauer

It was about the mid-1960s, and Pedro was feeling on top of the world; his two great passions in life were coming true. He was young, strong, and passionate about the sea; now he was going to sail as a cook aboard a fishing boat. Besides that, in recent months he had married his lovely girlfriend with the tender smile and sweet heavenly eyes.

His first sea voyage seemed to give wings to his dreams. The horizon seemed infinite to his gaze, and a sensation of happiness filled his thoughts. Pedro dreamed of exciting days to come and the exotic ports where his boat would soon be docking.

But boredom, an unvarying routine, and months of solitude at sea eventually wore him down. After a time his nautical fantasy of fortune was replaced by nocturnal phantoms of entrapment. Pedro remembers the day he got drunk for the first time at sea. He believed that drinking could help him escape, even for a few hours, from that dark liquid cloister. Over time, almost inadvertently, he became an alcoholic. He drank when he was onboard to cope with the daily routine; and he drank on land, as if by the irony of life he missed the never-ending rhythm of the waves.

Life gave him children and with that the responsibility of raising them. But Pedro had the devil in his body, so after working his daily shift he habitually ended up at the bar. His days were a heavy routine; dragging in late at night, he passed the remaining hours in a groggy stupor. The next morning, in a state of hangover, he stumbled out to wearily repeat his pattern of work and binge. It was inevitable that the day would come, and it surely did, when he could work no more. Pedro had become a total wreck.

One night Pedro had a dream. Childhood memories began to stir in his lonely heart. He had been raised in an Adventist family that believed in the second coming of Christ. That dream brought him in desperation to the point that he asked his wife to search for a religious instructor from her parent's church, somebody to teach him more about the Bible. Soon a young instructor came to visit, but after repeated occasions of finding Pedro always drunk at home, he stopped coming. It was as if Pedro had become an invisible man—invisible like the homeless, like the drug addicts, and like the alcoholics.

"They did not see me, they never looked me in my eyes, that's why they did not recognize me," exclaimed Richard Gere recently when he was filming a movie about the life of a vagabond on the streets of New York. Dressed as a vagabond, the actor spent hours without anyone recognizing him. He thought that within five minutes of initiating the filming someone would identify him and ruin the take. But no one looked into his eyes. It seems that many people do not have eyes capable of seeing beyond their own little world. But God has eyes and ears as well. His promise is: "Then you will call upon me and come and pray to me, and I will hear you" (Jeremiah 29:12, ESV).

Pedro had lost everything. He now could be seen lying in the gutters; still he did not stop drinking, and every cent he received from his small government pension was spent on booze. But in his night of anguish, in his Jacob night, he cried out to God: "Save me. Do whatever it takes to change me." He pleaded: "Do not hide Your face from me in the day of my trouble; incline Your ear to me; in the day that I call, answer me speedily" (Psalm 102:2, NKJV).

He prayed all night until he fell asleep on his knees. A few days later, Pedro felt a pain in his back and in his lower abdomen. He went to the hospital, where some tests were done, and his doctor said, "You have cancer in the prostate and kidneys. Your cancer is terminal; you have only a few months left."

Pedro's first reaction was, "Glory to God." He felt that the Lord was answering his prayer. It was like when Saul was knocked off his horse on the Damascus road (cf. Acts 9:1–6). Pedro realized that God had not forgotten him and that He was taking hold of his hand to lead him in the final days of his life. And, strangely, this conviction gave him power to stop drinking.

He began attending an Adventist church, and after a special Week of Prayer organized by the young people under the banner "Healing for Pedro"—to which friends, family, and other suffering folks were invited to come for prayers—Pastor Jose Maria Hage baptized him, and the first elder, Julio Chazarreta Sr., anointed him.

Pedro felt ready to die, and although his wife insisted he go for treatment to a naturopathic clinic in Chile in order to prolong his days, he refused. When the pastor and church elder visited him at his home and tried to convince him that going to the clinic would be a good plan, Pedro responded, "The treatment is expensive. I do not want to put more burdens on my family. Didn't you baptize me, Pastor? And didn't you anoint me, Brother Julio? Why should I do anything more? My life is in the Lord's hands. I told Him that if I can be useful for His purposes, He can prolong my days. And if not, fine, I am not afraid to die, because I know in whom I have believed."

When the church leaders left Pedro's house, they said to one another: "Poor Pedro, he is going to die, but how good it is that he accepted Jesus."

Six years later, Pedro was still very much alive. He was the missionary director of his new church, where the young instructor who years earlier had gone to his home was invited to give an evangelistic series. That young man was Julio Chazarreta Jr., today an evangelist working for *El Centinela*, our Spanish missionary magazine in North America. At the end of that series of meetings, thirty-eight people were baptized as a testimony that Christ heals both soul and body. Most of these people came to know Christ through Pedro's work and testimony. To date, that was the largest baptism to take place in the history of the church of Mar del Plata, Argentina.

Twenty years have gone by since that baptism, and Pedro Diaz is still alive, testifying to the healing power of Christ.

What does science say about health and happiness?

A few years ago an impressive study was conducted regarding the effects of physical activity on health. Researchers at Duke University Medical Center[1] recruited men and women ages fifty and older suffering from depression. They were divided into three groups at random. The first group was assigned four months of aerobic exercise; the second four months of antidepressant medication; and the third, both exercise and antidepressants. The exercise consisted of three weekly sessions of forty-five minutes of cycling or walking at moderate to high intensity. The results were surprising. After a period of four months, all three groups experienced a decrease in depression, had less dysfunctional attitudes, improved their self-esteem, and increased their happiness levels. It was found that exercise was as effective as the antidepressants, with the difference that exercise is cheaper and has no side effects. But there is something even more striking: six months after the participants had recovered from depression, those belonging to the first group had fewer relapses than those from the other groups. The name given to this study by the researchers was Standard Medical Intervention and Long-term Exercise (SMILE).

Physical activity reduces anxiety and stress; lowers the risk of many diseases (diabetes, colon cancer, and hypertension); strengthens bones, muscles, and joints; improves quality of life; and helps one sleep better and control weight.[2] In addition, research has shown that physical exercise is a most effective way to stimulate happiness.[3]

By contrast, it is also vital for good health to get daily and weekly rest. A recent study shows the importance of obedience to the fourth commandment given in the Old Testament for physical, mental, and spiritual health. In field studies, researcher Jerry W. Lee of Loma Linda University, California, says there is a direct link between the Sabbath day of rest and physical health and an indirect relationship between the observance of that day and a healthy lifestyle. He points to four factors that contribute to overall health: Sabbath rest, which increases the ability to cope with stress, promotes emotional and spiritual support by the church community, and develops social conditions to live an Adventist lifestyle; healthy eating; physical exercise; and abstinence from tobacco, alcohol, and drugs.[4]

Another interesting study, this one by Jama L. White, Amanda M. Blackburn, and Mary K. Plisco from the University of Richmond, Virginia, found more specifically the importance of Sabbath rest for physical and mental health in a consumer society, whose supreme law is productivity. The interesting thing about this study is its revelation of capitalist society's abandonment of the weekly rest (in this case, Sunday) and the strengthening that comes from the practice of Sabbath rest on the individual's capacity to cope with adversities in life. This is achieved only if the Sabbath becomes a day of "introspection and sanctification"; in other words, a day for a meaningful encounter with oneself and with God, not just a day for simply kicking back.[5]

Jesus and health

In chapter 5 of the Gospel of John a story is told about Jesus' visit to a sort of open-air hospital on the outskirts of Jerusalem. It was the Sabbath (verse 16), and this is not a minor detail.

The Divine Physician walked those corridors filled with suffering humanity. Finally, He stopped by the mat of one of the oldest patients in that establishment. It was a case of a man who had experienced thirty-eight years of disease and ineffective treatments. If medical records were kept, that patient's records would have listed failure after failure. A chronic case like his had no prospect of a cure. Why didn't Jesus pick an acute case? Those are the ones that respond best to treatment and offer the doctor greater professional satisfaction and success. But Jesus chose a chronic patient. Medical society generally does not want to spend money on chronic cases. Why waste time and resources on that which has no solution? Thankfully, however, Jesus did not think that way. He did not close the door of hope on the hopeless.

It is most striking to note Jesus' act of healing. He gave three specific prescriptions of great healing value, as if they were three capsules containing powerful medicine. The first was a question, the second a command, and the third a warning.

The question. "Do you want to get well?" (verse 6, NIV). It's a strange question for a chronic patient who has suffered for thirty-eight years. It almost seems ridiculous and could even be interpreted as a mockery. Nevertheless, that question contains much wisdom! Years of clinical observation have shown that, deep down, many who are chronically ill do not really want to be healed. Somehow they have become comfortable with the disease and may even experience some benefits from being disabled—no need to work, others will care for them, and people treat them kindly and give them preference in everything. Many patients complain of symptoms but make no effort to comply with treatment. Many alcoholics and drug addicts are not willing to change in order to escape the disease. They do not want to be cured. The first step to healing, therefore, is a fervent desire to be healthy and a disposition to forgo the "benefits" of dependence. If one does not really want to be healed, there is no reason to proceed to the second step. The unwilling patient condemns himself to continued suffering for the rest of his life.

The command. "Rise, take up thy bed, and walk" (verse 8, KJV). It is required of the patient to make an effort; he must abandon the horizontal and assume a vertical position, and he must take responsibility for his life thereafter. The mandate was not to give up but rather to march forward in continuous progress. Surrender is not an option; one must fight on. Clearly, Jesus saw willingness in this chronic patient to reach for new life. When Jesus was ready to help him take the first step, the paralytic replied, "Sir, I have no one to put me into the pool when the water is stirred up; and while I am going another steps down before me" (verse 7, ESV). The man spoke from frustration and failure, but somehow the light of hope and desire for change were kindled in him. For that reason Jesus gave the command.

The second step is not only having the desire but putting the willpower into action toward living a healthy lifestyle.

The warning. "See, you have been made well. Sin no more, lest a worse thing come upon you" (verse 14, NKJV). It is not enough to have a desire to change and to put into operation the necessary vital forces; one must go on to live in such a way that prevents relapse into the old ways. It is clear that health is linked to salvation, well-being, and happiness of spirit. Here, then, is where willpower comes into action. The paralytic had been the victim of intemperance and a self-destructive lifestyle. He had not learned or respected the laws of health. Now, after thirty-eight years of suffering its evils, the time had come to recognize that and embrace a life in harmony with the laws of health that God has provided for man's happiness.

When the power of the will is activated, divine grace intervenes to achieve the miracle.

How to achieve fullness of health

The Spanish word for health, *salud*, comes from the Latin *salus*, which also means "salvation." There is a very significant expression in the Spanish language, *sano y salvo* (literally, "healthy and safe" or "safe and sound" in common English expression). It would seem that both words have different meanings, but they are actually two very closely related terms that signal well-being or happiness. Both Spanish words have the same Latin root: *salvus*. Health, *salus*, is the quality of *salvus*, whole and intact. Hence the verb *salvere*: to feel good; the verb *salvare*: to save; and the noun *Salvatore*, which means "Savior."

In Hebrew just as in Greek (*soterios*) there exists the same relationship between the two words. *Health* is a synonym for *salvation*. Yet it is clear that health and salvation are not always interchangeable terms; consider, for example, that a believer in Christ might have the assurance of salvation but at the same time be suffering some serious disease. On the other hand, there are people without faith who might be in the very best of health. Bad weeds never die, as the saying goes. It doesn't always work out that a person who prays for healing receives that gift from God; and often it happens that a nonbeliever who mistreats his body still lives on to a very ripe old age. We must not forget that health also has to do with inherited propensities and genetic factors. But we can still do much to prevent disease and even counteract the negative effects on our bodies from what we have inherited through our genes.

God's health principles are simple and natural. If we obey them, we can add life to our years and years to our life. Through faith, the supernatural interacts with the natural. Along with salvation, God gives us health.

We cannot easily grasp that health and salvation are the same thing because in our minds we separate the natural order from the supernatural. We think of health as a matter of body and mind that has more to do with medicine, doctors, and hospitals. And we associate salvation with eternal life as promised to believers at the end of this mortal existence. But this division is not an accurate portrayal, for God's supernatural power is expressed both in the history of mankind and in nature. Quietly, but effectively, God acts to bestow health every day. And even more, He works to reconstruct our bodies despite the damage we inflict on them. The Creator is also the Sustainer of the universe. We are part of that universe. Most of the church faithful did not see the silent but effective action of God in the life of Pedro Diaz before his miracle of healing occurred.

Due to the fact that they could not see the supernatural action already taking place in Pedro, they were not able to give full credit to his words. But truthfully we can say that you and I, like all creatures, are part of the "natural order" with which the "supernatural" graciously interacts. We live in and with nature, never separate from it. The stars above, earth's flora and fauna here below, and all of humankind are God's creation. And the very power of God that acts to correct man-made pollution in nature is also at work within us to restore health and to save us, just as it happened in the life of Pedro.

The work of redemption is a silent and powerful work that has as its ultimate purpose the health of all creation, which has been affected by the entrance of evil. Paul stated "that the whole creation groans" for restored health (Romans 8:22). And the promise is that there will be healthy new heavens and earth.

In the Old Testament, salvation is often described as the space created by God in which life can flourish. The fertile land is given as a salvific act of God for the welfare of His people. Health also occurs when God frees His people from their enemies (Exodus 14:13, 14, 30).

In the New Testament, Jesus frees people from physical and spiritual ills and restores health to the community. Healing is an act of salvation and a tangible proof of the reality of the kingdom of God among men. When Christ comes into our lives, when God's Word lives in our midst, the sick are healed, people do not die young from preventable diseases, and the elderly live in health for many years. Salvation and health go hand in hand. Both terms belong to the same divine desire: "Beloved, I pray that you may prosper in all things and be healthy, even as your soul prospers" (3 John 2, WEB).

Finally, the most important thing: Jesus performed the miracle of healing for that paralytic on the Sabbath. He did so because He is "Lord of the Sabbath" (Matthew 12:8). He invites us to His rest, which is, in the broader sense, acceptance of His salvation aimed at the fullness of unending health: "Come unto me, all ye that labour and are heavy laden, and I will give you rest" (Matthew 11:28, KJV).

Thus, Jesus converted the Sabbath into a day of health and salvation. Science confirms the value of Sabbath rest for physical, mental, and spiritual health. And precisely because "the commandment is holy and just and good" (Romans 7:12, MEV), the Lord tells us to "remember the Sabbath day, to keep it holy" (Exodus 20:8, KJV). "Let us therefore labour to enter into that rest [the Sabbath of Christ], lest any man fall after the same example of unbelief" (Hebrews 4:11, KJV).

In this way you can give new life to your dreams.

Bible Teaching: Health and Jesus
(John 5:1–9)

Introduction

Hippocrates, the Greek physician considered to be the father of medicine, uttered a wise phrase that remains valid down to our day: "Let food be thy medicine and medicine be thy food."

At the pool of Bethesda, Jesus chose to heal a chronically ill man who perhaps had no hope of a cure. This shows us that Jesus is capable of working great miracles and that He goes in search of those without hope. But is that healing power reserved only for those who are suffering sickness?

Does the Word of God offer us counsel to prevent disease and stay healthy? Let's consider what the Bible says about health:

Does the Bible say that God is concerned about our health? *(3 John 2)*

The Bible says that God is interested in our physical, emotional, and spiritual well-being. Clearly, He wants us to live preventively so that it won't be necessary for Him to come running to our aid miraculously. Seeing as how God is concerned about our health, He provides counsel in order that we might prevent disease.

What is the relationship between physical health and spiritual health? *(1 Corinthians 6:19, 20)*

Since we are temples of the Holy Spirit, the care of our bodies glorifies the Creator. We glorify God because we are aware that life and health are a gift from God. This does not mean that disease is a sign that God has removed that gift; on the contrary, to care for our health means that we do not neglect that gift.

What is the relationship between our health, the food we consume, and spiritual life? *(1 Corinthians 10:31)*

All our actions have consequences. If we live for God, we live to glorify Him. What we eat and drink and our whole lifestyle expresses how much we value the gift of life He has given us.

What counsel does God give us about certain foods? *(Leviticus 11:3–20)*

Do not fall into error by thinking that salvation depends on whether we eat this or that food. We have already seen that salvation comes from Christ.

But once saved, we care for our bodies as an expression of gratitude to Him who created us and redeemed us in Jesus. This is the beginning of happiness. Without health we are not be happy or fulfilled.

What does the Lord counsel us about alcoholic beverages? *(Proverbs 23:31–34)*

The Lord advises us to avoid alcohol to avoid falling into drunkenness, which can lead us to ruin. A sober life is best for the health of body and soul and for the sake of our happiness.

How does God help us to obey His counsels? *(Ezekiel 36:27)*

The secret to living a sober life with temperance is in the grace of the Spirit of God. His grace gives us the power to acquire healthy lifestyle habits.

Through which Person does Jesus help us in our struggle for a healthy lifestyle? *(Galatians 5:22, 23)*

The Third Person of the Godhead, the Holy Spirit, enables us to gain self-control over our lifestyle habits.

Conclusion

Jesus healed the paralytic because He desires complete health for all of humanity. For that reason He gives us counsel for maintaining good health. If, however, for some reason we get sick, Jesus is the Divine Physician. We can go to Him for comfort and wisdom to face adversity. Bernard Le Bovier de Fontenelle said, "Health is the element that puts value in all of the zeros of life."

An appeal

Will you accept the grace of Jesus so that, by the power of the Holy Spirit, you can live a healthy lifestyle?

My resolve

I accept the grace of Jesus and want to live a healthy life through the power of the Holy Spirit.

I sign this in acceptance: _____.

Do I Live a Healthy Lifestyle?
Health Assessment

Take two minutes to determine whether you are doing things right in caring for your body and health. Review some of your daily habits. Respond honestly and discover how healthy your lifestyle is. The results can help you stay on the right track or help you make the appropriate changes as soon as possible.

Questions	A	B	C
1. Do you feel at one with your body?	Yes	Sometimes	No
2. Do you schedule at least one medical examination each year?	Yes	Sometimes	No
3. Do you do any activities to de-stress and relax?	Yes	Sometimes	No
4. Do you manage to get a good night's sleep regularly?	Yes	Sometimes	No
5. Do you go outdoors and get fresh air?	Yes	Sometimes	No
6. Do you smoke?	No	Sometimes	Regularly
7. Do you drink alcohol?	No	Sometimes	Regularly
8. Do you eat between meals?	No	Sometimes	Regularly
9. Do you live or work around cigarette smoke?	No	Sometimes	Yes
10. Do you take care to follow a healthy eating plan?	Yes	Sometimes	No
11. Do you consume fried foods and sweets?	No	2–3 times/week	A lot
12. How often do you perform physical activity?	2 or more times a week	Once a week	Infrequently
13. How many blocks per week do you usually walk?	15 or more	5–15	Less than 5
14. How would you assess your emotional life?	Positive	Acceptable	Negative
15. How would you evaluate your work routine?	Manageable	Intense	Stressful

Interpretation of your health assessment
Score your points for each answer: A = 10; B = 5; and C = 0.

Results

100 to 150 points: You lead a healthy life. Conserve those good habits. As the years pass, adapt your habits and intensify them.

50 to 95 points: Yours is a fairly healthy lifestyle, but you need to improve in some areas to achieve an ideal state. Identify your weaknesses and turn them around by adopting the health suggestions that can help maintain you in good health.

Fewer than 50 points: You are not preserving your health as you should if your goal is to live long and well. You have to convince yourself of the need for change. Consult a doctor. You need to recognize your physical condition and establish a healthful plan as soon as possible.

---

1. Michael Babyak et al., "Exercise Treatment for Major Depression: Maintenance of Therapeutic Benefit at 10 Months," *Psychosomatic Medicine* 62, no. 5 (September/October 2000): 633–638.

2. Emily B. Kahn et al., "The Effectiveness of Interventions to Increase Physical Activity: A Systematic Review," *American Journal of Preventive Medicine* 22, no. 4, suppl. 1 (May 2002): 73–107.

3. Stuart J. H. Biddle and Nanette Mutrie, *Psychology of Physical Activity: Determinants, Well-Being, and Interventions* (London: Routledge, 2002).

4. Devon J. Superville, Kenneth I. Pargament, and Jerry W. Lee, "Sabbath Keeping and Its Relationships to Health and Well-Being: A Mediational Analysis," *The International Journal for the Psychology of Religion* 24, no. 3 (June 2014): 241–256, doi: 10.1080/10508619.2013.837655.

5. Jama L. White, Amanda M. Blackburn, and Mary K. Plisco, "Rest as a Virtue: Theological Foundations and Applications to Personal and Professional Life," *Journal of Psychology and Theology* 43, no. 2 (Summer 2015): 98–120.

Chapter 6

Wisdom

We can rejoice, too, when we run into problems and trials, for we know that they help us develop endurance. And endurance develops strength of character, and character strengthens our confident hope of salvation. And this hope will not lead to disappointment. For we know how dearly God loves us, because he has given us the Holy Spirit to fill our hearts with his love.
—Romans 5:3–5, NLT

Miguel and Fortunato were two hill-country boys; they were inseparable brothers. During school vacations they helped their parents do farm work. When harvesttime came in the outlying regions of Mexico, their father would head out in search of work in order to provide for his family. Often he would be away for several weeks at a time. Meanwhile, his wife and children did not sit around idly; they also looked for work in a neighboring village. Fortunato and Miguel, along with their mother and sister, Aurelia, packed some clothes and food in preparation for their time away from home. The first thing they did when they reached the village was look for a place to lay their heads at night. There were so many people flocking in for seasonal employment that it was impossible to find rooms. With the harvest about to begin and so many people coming into the village, finding accommodations was always an uncertainty, but fortunately Fortunato came up with an idea: "Let's go camp in a cave I have seen in the hills not far from here."

After a brisk hike they located the cave and carefully inspected all of its nooks and crannies. They were glad to find it empty, so they got to work cleaning it as best they could, and then they gathered firewood and lit a protective fire for the approaching night. Lulled by the sound of a nearby stream, they soon fell into a weary sleep.

At dawn they headed out to work in the fields. But about midmorning, the sky filled with threatening, dark clouds, and heavy claps of thunder signaled a storm bearing down on them. Under a tremendous downpour they hastened back to their cave. Night fell, and it was still raining hard. The swollen stream became choked with brush and small creatures trying to escape. In the cave they were high and dry without any apparent cause for concern. They were warm and comfortable on their beds piled up with blankets.

The family slept peacefully until suddenly a horrendous noise reverberated off of the walls of the cave. They awoke in fright: What was that? It didn't sound like thunder. No, it was more like the roar of an angry beast! A flash of lightning lit up the silhouette of a huge figure standing upright at the entrance to the cave. It was a bear! Terrified, the four felt helpless and trapped.

Hurriedly, the mother lit a torch improvised with rags tied around the end of a branch and took a stand in front of her children. Fortunato did the same, advancing between his mother and the bear. Miguel joined his brother also. The bear rose menacingly on its hind legs and growled ferociously; it wanted to get back into its lair that these humans had taken over, but the heat of the flames deterred the beast from attacking.

The mother and the two boys countered every attempt of the bear to retake its cave. It was a life-or-death situation that kept them on their toes. Aurelia could do nothing but huddle in tears at the back of the cave. They knew they could not hold out very long against the bear, for they had only a small supply of firewood left. Would it be enough to last them all night? Fortunato and Miguel took turns with their mother keeping the fire going. Each time the flames started dying down, the bear moved in closer. When the last of the wood was reduced to mere embers, dawn began to break and the disgruntled bear finally decided to amble away. The family fell to their knees and, though still shaken by the ordeal, thanked God for saving their lives.

That night's struggle was a metaphor for the rest of their lives: they refused to give in and they kept the fire burning. After that experience, Fortunato and Miguel lived on as though gifted with a second chance at life. Every moment of their unforgettable experience charged them with lasting courage and inner strength. The confrontation with that danger taught the Herrera brothers that they should never surrender in the face of adversities.

As those two young men grew, their horizons broadened. Fortunato and Miguel decided to emigrate from Durango, in northern Mexico, to the United States.

In his homeland, Fortunato had learned his father's leather-working trade; he made saddles and saddle gear as well as sheaths for machetes, pouches, and holsters for rifles and pistols. He also drove a delivery truck, taking his wares on the road.

Both brothers arrived in California in the 1960s, but shortly afterward they separated. In 1968, Fortunato was living in Yerington, Nevada, doing agricultural work among the irrigation canals. Miguel stayed in California, and when he tried to join his brother, he was detained by the immigration authorities and deported. But as soon as he had crossed the border in San Luis Rio Colorado, Mexico, he turned around and returned to the United States, never to depart again.

Some twenty years later a new chapter opened up in the life of the Herrera brothers. In 1984, Miguel sold his truck to Fortunato. That day, Fortunato felt on top of the world and full of renewed youthful excitement for life. Such was his enthusiasm that he proposed to his brother Miguel that they form a trucking company. That meant they would have to borrow money and promise each other to work together diligently to make it a success. In 1985, they founded Herrera Brothers, Inc.

But adversity does not discriminate. Because of the financial depression of the United States in 2008, their previously successful enterprise went into bankruptcy. They were out on the street again, but they did not give up. Soon they established a machine shop in Payette, Idaho, and later that same year Fortunato began driving trucks again. Miguel had to wait another year before rejoining his brother. Since then the company has not stopped growing, and it now runs a fleet of trucks and trailers. They hire drivers and are prospering notably as they long-haul products far and wide on the nation's highways.

As I write these lines seated in Miguel's beautiful country home, surrounded by fields of wheat and corn in southern Idaho, with a view of the Payette River, I ask what his secret was that allowed him to successfully overcome adversity.

"I know people who have been through a lot tougher things in life to achieve their dreams. They are the real champions. Ours was more like a comfortable ride. But I can say I've learned some things along the way. For example, failures teach more than successes. No one learns through pleasure but instead through pain. We never stop learning, because life never ceases to teach. In times of crisis we learn the value of things and friends. When you're up, your friends know who you are. When you're down, only then do you really know who your friends are."

"After the financial crisis of 2008, what did you learn?"

"Well, I learned many things. For example: Do not spend first and then save what is left over, instead save first and then spend what is left over. Do not get into what you do not know. For example: Do not play the stock market because the winner is always the one who manages your money; not you. Put your efforts into hard work; not speculation. Practice honesty in all your business dealings. It's a good idea to diversify so that you have several sources of income and won't have to depend on just one option. And if you fail in one thing, there's always a good chance you will get back on your feet. Remember that it is not good to take many risks. There is a saying, 'You shouldn't measure the depth of the river with both feet.' "

"What was your source of power in the midst of failure?"

"Faith and hope in Christ."

"And your greatest satisfaction?"

"I would say that to know God keeps His promises is my greatest satisfaction. In life's crises I have learned that we can be stripped of everything at any time, but we can get on in life by helping others. When we were broke, we never stopped giving offerings and tithes to the church. Although it seems contradictory, that act of selflessness made us less impoverished, because it energized us spiritually to face the future. Giving back to God what belongs to Him and helping others in need are two sides of the same coin. God owns the world and everything in it. He gave us power and dominion over all things and asks us to return only ten percent of our wealth to Him. The more generous we were, the better off we became. This is God's promise: 'Bring ye all the tithes into the storehouse, that there may be food in my house; and prove me now herewith, saith the LORD of hosts, if I will not open you the windows of heaven, and pour you out a blessing' " (Malachi 3:10, KJV).

Meanwhile, Fortunato, sitting beside me on the couch, listened intently to his brother's comments. When I asked whether he wanted to add something more to their story, he told me about his conversion:

"I came to know Christ in the 1970s, through the messages of Pastor George Vandeman, speaker of the television program *It Is Written*. When at that time my brother visited me in Nevada, I was surprised that he did not work on Saturdays. When I asked him why he kept the seventh day of the week, Miguel told me about the fourth commandment. I didn't know anything about it. After studying the Bible, my wife Lucia and I decided to accept the gospel of Christ's grace and obey the Ten Commandments. The weekly Sabbath rest was a great gift for us as we faced life's demands. Knowing that every week there is a day of rest is something comforting for the body and soul."

Despite adversities in their adult lives, the Herrera brothers did not give up, just as they did not fail to stand bravely when faced by the bear back when they were five and six years old. At that earlier time they raised a burning torch of fire, and in their later experience of financial crisis, they raised the inspired torch of the Word of God, which illuminates the path of the believer, as the psalmist says, "Your word is a lamp to my feet and a light to my path" (Psalm 119:105, MEV). They clung to the Word and kept their faith intact. There is no greater source of truth outside the Bible. This Book is both divine and human, as is Christ. Holy men of God wrote under the Inspiration of the Holy Spirit (see 2 Timothy 3:16; 2 Peter 1:21).

All Christian doctrine is found in the Bible, and great wisdom for learning to live in its light emanates from this Book. All of human history takes on deeper meaning in the context of the history of salvation recorded in Scripture. In its pages God is made known, along with an understanding of His plan of redemption. All sixty-six books of the Bible speak of the love and justice of God, of Christ and His grace, and of the sanctifying power of the Holy Spirit. The reader of the Bible becomes wise through practicing its sanctifying teachings. Happiness comes to those who share its truths.

The Herrera brothers represent the fulfilled dreams of millions of immigrants who with effort and sacrifice have made this country great. They work hard, and many have learned to enjoy the Sabbath rest. They have found that honest work and good management are rewarded and that faith in Christ has a much higher reward: eternal life.

What science says about how to face adversity

In a study based on women with advanced cancer, it was found that patients who sought the support of family and friends as a strategy to face adversity had a better defense system and achieved a much higher survival rate than those who resigned themselves to their fate in isolation and depression.[1]

It is difficult to make sense of a traumatic event, such as having had a serious illness, having experienced the death of a family member, or having suffered a violent robbery. However, it was found that those who had lost a loved one and were able to come to grips with it, making rational sense of it, showed less depression and fewer symptoms of post-traumatic stress disorder (PTSD) within a year of that loved one's death. For example, a participant in that study stated, "I think my father's illness was something that had to happen and was part of the divine plan." This attitude is shown to contribute to emotional recovery much more rapidly than is the case among those who consider such occurrences illogical or arbitrary.[2]

Depression clearly does not help us face adversity, but faith does help overcome our depressive moments in life. In this regard, a recent study by the London School of Economics and Political Science, United Kingdom, reported that "participation in religious activities is related to a decrease in depression symptoms for up to four years subsequently." Specifically, the research was conducted on 9,068 people more than fifty years old from Austria,

Belgium, Denmark, France, Germany, Italy, Spain, Sweden, Switzerland, and the Netherlands. It was found that those involved in religious organizations had better mental health than those involved primarily in sports activities or social clubs or those engaged in politics (activists in this third category were the most stressed and depressed). Those who devoted one day of the week to worshiping God showed better results in the long term.

According to the epidemiologist Mauricio Avendaño, one of the authors of the study, the church seems to play a very important role in keeping depression at bay, and faith is the best defense mechanism in periods of disease. He concluded that religion influences one's way of life and the social bonds that are formed—helping to prevent loneliness—and it generates defense mechanisms against stress.[3]

Jesus and adversity

In Matthew 6:25–34, we find what we might call "a list of resources to cope with adversity." These texts prescribe Jesus' practical counsel for coping with the stress and anxiety common to the problems people face. There are five basic prescriptions:

1. *Become active, cease incessant worrying.* It is a call not to allow ourselves to be dominated by anxiety but instead to deal directly with the real problem at hand.

2. *Change the direction of your focus.* Observe the birds up above and the lilies of the field, recommends the Master (verses 26, 28). In other words: stop looking inward and making yourself out to be a victim of all the evils that happen to you. Self-pity weakens us.

3. *Have faith.* This is the challenge of learning to place your problems in God's hands after having done what you can to solve them.

4. *Define your priorities.* Put your values in proper order. The first and most important thing to do is to "seek ye first the kingdom of God and His righteousness"; after that all other things will fall into their proper places (verse 33, KJV).

5. *Live one day at a time.* "Sufficient unto the day is the evil thereof" (verse 34, KJV). Do not overburden today with the concerns of tomorrow.

These are wise and important principles to help us face the adversities of everyday life, whatever the degree of difficulty we may be hit with. However, it seems that life has no resources to confront the greatest adversary, death. What other adversity is more powerful than death, whether that of a loved one or our own?

Jesus also has an answer for death. Let's turn to the fourth Gospel. The book of John is one of signs (*símata* in Greek). The apostle says: "And truly Jesus did many other signs in the presence of His disciples, which are not written in this book; but these are written that you may believe that Jesus is the Christ, the Son of God, and that believing you may have life in His name" (John 20:30, 31, NKJV). What tremendously good news that is—believing in Jesus, we can face down and overcome death!

What are the signs that John mentions?

John records seven signs that Jesus performed:

1. He turned water into wine (2:1–12).
2. He healed the son of a government official (4:46–54).
3. He healed the paralytic of Bethesda (5:1–18).
4. He fed a multitude (6:1–15).
5. He walked on the sea (6:16–21).
6. He gave sight to a man born blind (9:1–34).
7. He raised Lazarus from the dead (11:1–44).

The first sign is the key to explaining the other signs. The transformation of water into wine encapsulates an essential teaching concerning salvation. The water represents the natural and ordinary, while the fruit of the vine is a symbol of the blood of Christ: it points to His death and to salvation (1 Corinthians 11:25, 26).

To be saved there must be a transformation; the natural life must become a spiritual life, as in the miracle of the water that became wine. This transformation is made possible by faith. Indirectly, that was what Jesus said to the official who came asking Him to heal his dying son. Jesus chided: "Unless you see signs and wonders, you will not believe" (John 4:48, MEV). The officer was looking for a miracle before he would believe, and Jesus wanted him to understand that first of all it was necessary to exercise faith. There was a change in the man's thinking that then made it possible for Jesus to respond to the plea of faith and save the boy's life. As we saw in the previous chapter, the paralytic of Bethesda also had to exercise faith before he could rise up and walk. Faith transforms and multiplies, like the loaves and fish that Jesus fed to the crowd. "If you can believe, all things are possible to him who believes" (Mark 9:23, MEV).

But what is the meaning of the last and decisive sign of Jesus Christ? It is the one that completes perfectly all of the other signs, the superlative miracle of Jesus that gives us every reason to believe in His name and to trust His promise of eternal life. For that reason, it is so very important.

In chapter 11 of John we read that there was in Bethany a young man named Lazarus, who had two sisters, Mary and Martha. Mary was the one

84

Give Life to Your Dreams

who washed Jesus' feet and anointed Him with perfume at Simon's house (verse 2). The Gospel narrative might suggest the idea that both sisters were older and filled a motherly role regarding their younger brother. Perhaps for this reason no mention was made of Lazarus when Jesus was at the family home. We only come to know this young man during his illness that caused such anguish to his sisters. Lazarus was allowed to die, and Jesus made no move to come to the family's side for four days. Obviously, this was pre-ordained "for the glory of God, that the Son of God may be glorified through it" (verse 4, NKJV). By this strategy the Master was to undeniably demonstrate to everyone that He is "the resurrection and the life"; and he who believes in Him, "though he die, yet shall he live" (verse 25, RSV).

The story of the resurrection of Lazarus is one of the most impressive and emotional events of the Bible. Jesus arrived at the height of mourning. An atmosphere of deep emotion and sorrow hung over the scene. A group of family and friends had gathered around the sisters to comfort them. The entry of Jesus and His disciples brought some expectation. Speaking with Martha, the Master was moved and shed memorable tears. Then He asked to see the tomb where Lazarus had been placed. Upon reaching the site, which was a cave, He ordered that the stone be rolled aside, exposing the open burial chamber with its noticeably decomposing content. At that point, He raised a prayer to His heavenly Father in order to make clear to everyone present the purpose of the miracle about to take place: "That they will believe that you sent me" (verse 42, CEB). "Having said this, Jesus shouted with a loud voice, 'Lazarus, come out!' The dead man came out, his feet bound and his hands tied, and his face covered with a cloth. Jesus said to them: 'Untie him, and let him go' " (verses 43, 44, CEB), He called to the very dead Lazarus, and what had been a lifeless cadaver came out of the grave fully alive, to the utter astonishment and boundless joy of many of those present.

Jesus' signs exercise opposing effects on those who witness them. To those of faith, they constitute an extraordinary sensation of joy and awe in the presence of God's power, but to those whose hard hearts refuse to believe, they produce anger and hatred. There were among the witnesses to the raising of Lazarus certain priests and spies who took no pleasure in what they had just seen. They went away from that holy ground to plot the murder of both Jesus and Lazarus (John 11:45–57; 12:9–11).

The name Lazarus comes from the Hebrew and means "God's help." It is a popular form of the Hebrew *Elazar:* "God has helped." It is applied to one who has been helped by God; in the case of Lazarus, he was helped out of the tomb and restored to life and health.

Today, God wants to help you to believe in Jesus, "the resurrection and the life" (John 11:25), so that with faith placed in Him you may face the greatest of all adversities in your existence: mortality.

Coping with adversity

We all have to face problems and deal with adverse circumstances. Facing adversity intelligently not only allows us to move forward but can even become a source of happiness.

How can you be happier when you're going through illness, bereavement, the death of a spouse, poverty, or the like? It is not easy, but it is possible. Transform your crisis through dealing with it cognitively. What today is a crisis that causes you to suffer, tomorrow can become your success story of deep personal satisfaction and renewal. Studies and experience have shown that the happiest people are those who have learned to endure trials without being overcome by them. It all depends on how the difficulties are addressed or coped with.

The term used in psychology to express the ability to overcome adversity or to deal with stress is *coping*. *Coping* can be defined as facing the enemy; facing a danger, problem, or compromising situation. This is what we do to relieve the pain, stress, and suffering caused by an unfortunate event or a negative situation. There are different ways of coping. Scholars basically distinguish two: focus on emotions and flee in desperation in order to escape the discomfort; or focus on the problem and seek solutions to help overcome it. In other words, you can overcome difficulties and derive something positive from them, or you can allow yourself to be overcome by adversity and simply succumb to it.

The Bible says: "All things work together for good to those who love God" (Romans 8:28, MEV). How is it possible that a tragedy can produce a good outcome? The German philosopher Friedrich Nietzsche said: "What does not kill me makes me stronger." How can it be that suffering a calamity makes one stronger? What this amounts to is finding the silver lining in the dark storm clouds of life. It is to see the positive side of misfortune, to find something redemptive in a loss or a negative event. Here are some tips that can be of help:

Write expansively about your experience. This can help you make sense of your misfortune. Several years ago the psychologist James Pennebaker undertook research on the health benefits of writing out one's traumatic experience. He studied the cases of many people who had been encouraged to describe for about fifteen to thirty minutes the details of their painful experiences. He also asked them to continue composing additional insights into their experiences during the following three to five days. The results of people who expressed their trauma in writing were compared by him to another group who wrote about random nonrelated topics. He found striking differences. Those who spent three days writing out and analyzing their deep feelings, in subsequent months came less often to seek professional counseling, their immune systems worked better, they showed less depression and afflictions, they earned higher grades in classes, and they fared much better at their jobs.[4]

Discuss your problem with trusted friends. Share your painful experience with someone you know, communicate your emotions, and try to better understand what happened. Maybe your marriage failed because you fell into a depression that you just could not overcome, or you dedicated too much time to your job and forgot about your spouse, or there was some adverse circumstance of life that was not foreseen. It is important to reflect on your growth and recovery progress after your loss. Do you sense that you're more compassionate or grateful or sensitive or tolerant of others? In what manner might you have gained more strength from having passed through this situation?

Take time to spend with God. Set aside, as the commandment indicates, the Sabbath day for closeness with Him (see Exodus 20:8–11). Talk with God every day and seek to find answers for your soul in the Bible. You will not always find what you need immediately, but eventually new ways of seeing things will open up your mind. You will discover that what happened, painful though it was, also presents some positive elements that result in various unexpected benefits.

Bible Teaching: Jesus and Adversity
(John 11:17–44)

Introduction

There is a story in the Bible about an event that occurred shortly after the death of the prophet Elisha. Armed bands of Moabites were ravaging the land of Israel. One day some folks set out to bury a man when suddenly they saw a group of menacing Moabites. Hurriedly, they heaved the body into a nearby cave where Elisha's remains had been deposited. When the cadaver landed on Elisha's bones, the man revived and stood to his feet (see 2 Kings 13:20, 21). This is the power of God, a foretaste of the general resurrection to come. There wasn't anything magical about those bones, but the Spirit of God wanted to teach Israel's enemies that though Elisha had died, his God never dies; nor does He abandon His faithful people.

One of the most extraordinary miracles of all time, as we have already seen, was that which Jesus performed in benefit of Lazarus. But had Lazarus really died? Do we humans really die, or are our souls immortal? What is death?

Let us consider what the Bible says about the state of the dead:

How was man created in this world? *(Genesis 2:7; 1:27)*

To understand what death is, we must first understand how God created man. God formed man of the dust of the ground and breathed into his nostrils the breath of life. In other words, man is not just dust or breath. He is the union of those two elements: breath and dust. If one of these elements is missing, there is no life. It is important to note that life in this world is a miracle of God.

What is death? *(Ecclesiastes 12:7; Psalm 146:4)*

Death could be defined as the separation of the two elements that make up life.

Is the soul immortal according to the Bible? *(Ezekiel 18:4)*

Perhaps because of our Greco-Roman cultural background, we have assigned the word *soul* an interpretation that the Greeks and Romans employed. However, the Bible sees *soul* quite differently. It is a word derived from the Hebrew expression *nephesh*, which means "to be alive." In other words, the human being is a "soul" while living. When he dies, he ceases to be a soul.

What is the state of the dead? *(Ecclesiastes 9:5, 6)*

According to the Bible, the dead are in a state of complete unconsciousness.

They do not hear nor see nor live. Jesus compared the death of Lazarus with sleep (John 11:11–13).

What question did the patriarch Job ask about death? *(Job 14:14)*
Job's question was and is the same question asked by millions of human beings. And it is, of all possible questions, the most important—the one most anxiously awaiting an answer.

What does the Bible say about the hope of returning to life after death? *(John 11:24)*
People who lived during Jesus' time knew the concept of resurrection. The idea of returning to life after death is biblical.

What did Jesus say about His power over death? *(John 11:25; Revelation 1:18)*
Jesus has supreme authority over death, and He can resurrect whomever He wants.

Conclusion
During His ministry, Jesus raised several people: the daughter of a Jewish leader named Jairus, she died mere minutes before Jesus arrived at her bedside; the son of a widow from the village of Nain, who died several hours previous to Jesus' approach and was brought back to life while lying on a stretcher heading to the cemetery; and finally, Lazarus, who had died several days before Jesus reached the burial place. Jesus' power was *in crescendo* during His ministry on earth. When He returns, He will go much further and raise the millions of believers who have been in their graves for centuries and millennia (1 Thessalonians 4:16, 17). Erich Sauer said: "The cross is the victory, the resurrection the triumph. . . . The resurrection is the public display of the victory, the triumph of the Crucified One."[5]

An appeal
Will you accept the grace of Jesus and trust His promise of resurrection?

My resolve

I accept the grace of Jesus and His promise that fills me with hope and comfort in the face of my own mortality.

I sign this in acceptance: _____.

How Well Can I Handle Stress?
Evaluation of My Capacity to Cope

The following are ways of thinking and behaving that people often use to deal with problems or stressful situations that occur in life. To answer, read each one of the ways of coping carefully and remember how many times you have recently used any of these resources. Make a mark on the number that best represents the degree to which you employed each one of the ways of coping with stress, according to the following scale:

0=Never 1=Few times 2=Sometimes 3=Frequently 4=Almost always

	How do you generally behave in stressful situations?	0	1	2	3	4
1	I try to analyze the causes of the problem in order to deal with it.					
2	I try to solve the problem following well thought-out steps.					
3	I establish an action plan and try to follow it.					
4	I talk to the people involved to find a solution to the conflict.					
5	I face the problem by implementing several specific solutions.					
6	I am convinced that no matter what I do, things will always go wrong.					
7	I do not do anything concrete, because there will always be problems.					
8	I understand that I am the main cause of the problem.					
9	I feel helpless and unable to do something positive to change the situation.					
10	I realize that by myself I can do nothing to solve the problem.					
11	When problems come to my mind, I try to concentrate on other things.					
12	I concentrate on work or other activities to forget the problem.					
13	I go out to the movies, to dinner, to drive around, etc., to forget the problem.					
14	I try not to think about the problem.					
15	I practice a sport to forget the problem.					

16	I attend church.					
17	I ask for spiritual help from a religious person or a trusted friend.					
18	I go to church and pray that the problem will be resolved.					
19	I have faith that God will remedy the situation.					
20	I pray.					

Results and interpretation of the evaluation of my capacity to cope

There are many ways to deal with problems that can be either positive or negative, as is explained below.

1. *A focus on the resolution of the problem.* This is an excellent way of coping. The *higher* the average, the better. To find your level, add up the points for questions 1 to 5.

> *Low: 0 to 5 points; medium: 6 to 15 points; and high: 16 to 20 points.*

2. *Negative self-targeting.* This is a harmful coping style. The *lower* the average, the better. To find your level, add up the points for questions 6 to 10.

> *Low: 0 to 5 points; medium: 6 to 15 points; and high: 16 to 20 points.*

3. *Avoidance.* This is not a beneficial way to cope with stress, although sometimes it can be useful. It is best to have a *low* or *medium* average. To find out your level, add up the points for questions 11 to 15.

> *Low: 0 to 5 points; medium: 6 to 15 points; and high: 16 to 20 points.*

4. *Religious support.* This is a very good coping style. The *higher* the average, the better. To find out your level, add up the points for questions 16 to 20.

> *Low: 0 to 5 points; medium: 6 to 15 points; and high: 16 to 20 points.*

---

1. David Spiegel et al., "Effect of Psychosocial Treatment on Survival of Patients With Metastatic Breast Cáncer," *Lancet* 334, no. 8668 (October 1989): 888–891, doi: 10.1016/S0140-6736 (89)91551-1.

2. Christopher G. David, Susan Nolen-Hoeksema, and Judith Larson, "Making Sense of

Loss and Benefiting From the Experience: Two Construals of Meaning," *Journal of Personality and Social Psychology* 75, no. 2 (August 1998): 561–574, doi: 10.1037/0022-3514.75.2.561.

3. "Depresión," psiquiatría.com, accessed August 13, 2015, http://www.psiquiatria.com /depresion.

4. James W. Pennebaker, *Opening Up: The Healing Power of Expressing Emotions* (New York: The Guilford Press, 1997).

5. Erich Sauer, *The Triumph of the Crucified: A Survey of Historical Revelation in the New Testament*, trans. G. H. Lang (London: Paternoster Press, 1951), 32, http://www.despatch.cth .com.au/Books_V/erichsauer2.htm.

Chapter 7

Faith and Religious Practice

A growing current in the science of psychology suggests that
religious people are happier, healthier and recover better
from trauma than people who are not religious.
—Sonja Lyubomirsky

Lindorfo Giménez-Giménez, better known as Fito, was born on September 8, 1950, in Oviachic, Sonora, Mexico. In the wee hours of that Friday, little Fito's inaugural cry resounded in every corner of the camp where his father worked on the construction of a dam. Mr. Giménez was a carpenter and had built the makeshift housing without knowing that this was where his child would be born. His wife, who came from another Giménez line, dedicated herself to raising their children. That morning she had given birth to the fourth child in a total of nine.

After a couple of years when the dam was completed and the rising waters covered the old village of Oviachic (which was reborn upriver on higher ground), the Giménez family moved on, looking for work along the US–Mexico border, more precisely in San Luis Rio Colorado, Sonora. Fito recalls the words passed on to him from family history, which had been spoken precisely on the day that they had left the dam. As they were leaving the site, his father got out of the truck carrying them away and looked at the river that had taken the town, and with it so many memories, and said: "Life is like that river; nothing resists the passage of time. So we have to quicken our pace."

And quicken the pace they did. Mr. Giménez soon found work as hired help for a rancher on the US side of the Colorado River. Fito remembers his peaceful early childhood and the afternoons in Somerton, Arizona, which were endlessly boring in that baking desert during all four seasons of the year. Although the locals said there were only two seasons: winter and hell.

Even before he was ten, Fito would go with his father on Saturdays to harvest cotton to earn a little money; he especially wanted to be able to buy his mother a gift when May 10 rolled around. Young Fito managed to earn more and more. In the early sixties, San Luis Rio Colorado was becoming a smaller version of Las Vegas, and Fito would cross over to peddle whatever trinkets and cheap souvenirs he could make a dime or quarter off of by hitting up the Americans who flocked over the border to visit Mexican bars and theaters. At that time there were also numerous well-off Mexicans coming into town. Fito's brash pestering of tourists with his trade brought him to the attention of the police. He was just eleven when officers were chasing him through the streets of San Luis whenever they saw him. If caught, Fito would end up at the police station overnight and wouldn't be released until he had shined all the officers' shoes the next morning.

When Fito turned fourteen years old, his father "arranged his papers" (formalized his immigration status). Then Fito felt more at ease to come and go across the border, and as we shall see, this would determine his fate. By then Humberto, the eldest Giménez son, had a *compadre* (close friend) in Sinaloa, a state famous for the production of marijuana. With that friendship began a "family business": Humberto soon contacted Mexican smugglers interested in trafficking marijuana into the United States. And in less time than it takes a rooster to crow, Humberto and his *compadre* (a mobster by profession) enrolled other Giménez siblings in the enterprise: Agustín, two years older than Fito; Evangelina, their only sister; and José Luis, the youngest. And since Fito liked money so much it wasn't difficult for Evangelina to convince him to serve as the "mule" to smuggle drugs across the river. At fourteen he was untouchable.

"Back then the American border guards were very nice," says Fito. And he took advantage of their easygoing ways to pass cars through with their trunks full of "bricks" (marijuana compacted into the shape of bricks). In time the American inspectors got savvier, and it was necessary to come up with more ingenious ways to pass the product without it being detected: it was packed into crannies around the motor and in the chassis or in the tires. Eventually, when it became too complicated to take it by land, they began smuggling it over via the Colorado River.

Having hurried the pace, in a few months the business grew in geographic proportions. Evangelina and Fito took care of business on the Mexican side of the river, growing, collecting, and transferring the marijuana to Arizona. And José Luis and Humberto handled business on the American side: expanding the market, transporting the drug to different cities, and receiving the money. In the beginning, they were supplied by Pedro Avilés, the "Chapo Guzmán" of the time, but then they bought a plane; and with their private pilot, Fito and Evangelina visited the Sierra de Chihuahua and Sinaloa, which borders Sonora, where even today marijuana is cultivated.

By then, Evangelina, known far and wide as "la Doña" (the Madam), had risen to ownership and become the head of the business. Her word was final, she made the deals and decided the strategies. There was a definite cruelty and abusiveness in her character, so much so that Agustín ended up leaving the family business and setting himself up independently. Fito stuck with Evangelina and was her right-hand man.

The drug market was spreading like a prairie fire carried on the wind: Tucson, Phoenix, Los Angeles, San Francisco, and Chicago. If they fulfilled by the ton, then they went farther: New York and Florida. As the business grew, the old ways of smuggling by "mule" became obsolete. Now they smuggled as much as they wanted by trucks, trains, airplanes, and ships. They simply bought the borders.

By now Fito was twenty years old. Those seemed to be glorious times. Things were going well for him financially and romantically; the flow of dollars was like the waters of Niagara, and he fell in love with a lovely brown-eyed beauty whom he stole from a poor country farmer. Five years later, on December 19, 1975, the couple legalized their civil status, and Virginia Rivera became Mrs. Virginia Giménez

Fito thought he had it all: family and money. What he didn't know is that "the love of money is the root of all evil" (1 Timothy 6:10, KJV). He owned houses, properties of all kinds, beautiful women, and, most importantly, the cooperation of the authorities. His fortune bought everyone: judges, police, lawyers, border officials, and anyone else needing to have their palms greased. This young man possessed everything, but he did not possess himself.

With so much money, Fito began to believe in the lie he was living. Because he felt strong, he turned violent; and all others fell to their knees before him. Fito knew that people were afraid of him because the authorities protected him. That security turned him into a despot. No one could touch him; it seemed that not even bullets could riddle him. Power is intoxicating and makes us feel superhuman, but in reality we are worthless. The oppressor would not be so strong if he didn't have accomplices among the oppressed themselves. Complicity is born from the fear of power and force, and it feeds on ignorance. Through ignorance dominance is greater and lasts longer than force.

Finally, in the 1970s, things began to go south precipitously for Fito. Until then, a certain mob lawyer named Garcia would arrange cover for all of his criminal conduct. Whenever he was taken into custody, Fito would just laugh in the face of the police. He never faced a courtroom. Until one day the countdown began: Agustín, his older brother, had killed a DEA agent on Mexican soil. "Ever since that day, we had the Feds all over us," recounts Fito.

In December 1972, in Tucson, Arizona, the FBI set up a trap for him, and this time he went to court. Fito was sentenced to seven years in prison for drug possession and conspiracy. At that time, the US Congress had voted into law the Conspiracy Act against all drug traffickers who, even without residence on US soil, produced and marketed drugs within the United States. But Fito appealed the sentence, and the law firm of Peter and Rose took the case to the San Francisco Federal Court of Appeals, where he managed to win the case. He spent only eleven months in prison in Lompoc, California.

But back in Mexico he wasn't quite so lucky. By then, la Doña had been sentenced to forty-three years in prison, Agustín had been murdered months earlier in San Luis Rio Colorado, and Humberto was in a wheelchair, having been seriously wounded in a shoot-out. The family no longer had any power to protect him. Fito went to prison. He was locked up from 1976 to 1980 in Nogales, Sonora. Even so, he did receive one appreciable favor: his brother Agustín, days before he was killed, had paid the authorities not to torture him. And Fito still had a political wedge he could play: the governor of Sonora was his cousin on both his mother's and his father's sides of the family.

After leaving Mexico in early 1980, Fito returned to the United States. He no longer had money because his lawyers had consumed most of it; and the money he had left in Mexico, hyperinflation had turned into wallpaper. Reduced to poverty, he began working in the lettuce harvest in California. Once again the FBI snagged him in another trap. Back in court, he was sentenced, in April 1982, to five years in prison. Now Fito had dangling over him the possibility of definitive deportation.

The sheriff who was transporting him to prison stopped in Palm Springs off Interstate 10 and told the prisoner that he was going to leave him there in police custody overnight, as that was as far as his jurisdiction extended. He told Fito that another official would pick him up the following day and take him to the prison in Riverside.

That was a night of great mental anguish for Lindorfo Giménez. He thought it might be a setup to murder him. He was completely alone in a cell. The officer on duty handed him a Bible, and Fito opened it to the Gospel of John and began to read. Until then nothing and nobody had ever touched him inside to change his conduct, but that night the Holy Spirit came to him. It was not a very pleasant visit—quite the opposite. It was a visit that subjected him to deep anguish. All night he wept and sought God. And, as in the night of Jacob's trouble (Genesis 32:24), at dawn Fito at last found peace. He knew that the worst was yet to come: jail and deportation. But now he began to feel an inner strength that up until then he had never known. In the very place where he feared he might leave his bones, he experienced rebirth.

* * * * *

Lindorfo began to share this story with me the night of January 4, 1996, twenty years ago. He added the final details on January 26 of that same year, while I was packing my suitcase to return to Buenos Aires, Argentina, where I lived at that time. I had gone for the first time to visit the harvest fields of Arizona, and there Virginia and Lindo, as I started calling him at that time, opened the door of their home to me and, not long after, also their hearts.

I write these lines on October 4, 2015. A week ago I called Lindo to clarify some facts of his story and ask how he was feeling now at this stage in life.

"What happened in the prison at Riverside, California, after that night of agony in Palm Springs?"

"The Lord continued to visit me. My repentance was profound, and that stage of it lasted many months. Palm Springs that night was just the beginning. While reading a Bible given to me by a group of Pentecostal brothers, I experienced again the presence of the Holy Spirit. It is a gift that He comes and confronts you with what you really are. I was proud of myself; and when God touched me, I saw what I really was: a coward who took advantage of people's weaknesses. When I came to this realization, I cried many nights; not out of fear for the consequences of my mistakes but because of the image I saw of myself in the Holy Spirit's mirror. No one had ever confronted me with such a picture of my life, and I felt disgusted with myself. I identified a lot with Paul's conversion and read chapter 9 of the Acts of the Apostles over and over again."

"Did anything reaffirm your faith while you were in prison?"

"When I arrived at my cell, my first thought was of my mother. She was suffering heart problems. I had asked the judge to sentence me after May 10, so that I could go and spend the last Mother's Day with her, but he did not. That night I prayed to God for her healing so that she would live to see me free again. God answered that plea: my mother lived another twenty years."

"What is the church for you?"

"It gave me faith, and with that came everything else. There is a church militant and a church triumphant. I belong to the militant one, because I long for the day when I can belong to the triumphant one. I am weak, and every day I die in Christ [see 1 Corinthians 15:31]. I cannot bear all my burdens alone, but Christ strengthens me [see Philippians 4:13]. The church is my family, my city of refuge. It is the place where sinners meet to seek the grace of Christ. To serve in the church is the engine of my life, because its message is the one that gave meaning and mission to my existence."

"What do you thank God for?"

"I'm grateful to God for the way He guided me. My past was the price I had to pay to gain hope. I would never have known Christ if not for my time in jail. In my earlier life there was no one to bring me close to God. But while I regret a lot of bad things I did, I do not regret the road that led me to meet the Lord. I am also grateful that my mother and my sister Evangelina accepted faith in Christ before they died. And I thank God for the faith of my children and my niece, Evangelina's daughter, who also accepted Christ."

* * * * *

Lindorfo was released from prison on July 3, 1985. He was imprisoned for twenty-six months; for good behavior his time was reduced by half. He was baptized on July 21, 1985, into the Seventh-day Adventist Church. When he was released, he founded a church in the Yuma prison.

I met Lindo five and a half years after his baptism and stayed at his home in the desert for a month. What surprised me most about him was his devotion to the Lord. Every morning he would gather his family around the table to pray and study the Word of God. After breakfast he headed out under the sun and the heat of the desert to put in an honest day's work at his auto mechanic shop, earning very little money. Seeing that, I wondered how long he would be able to bear a poor man's lifestyle when not long ago he had thousands of dollars in his pockets every day. Time gave the best answer.

After leaving prison, Lindorfo had yet to face a hearing before immigration officials. After receiving testimony from the Adventist pastor about how valuable Lindo was to his church and community, a favorable decision was reached. Today he is the most influential leader in the Mexicali Seventh-day Adventist Church in Baja California, Mexico. He lives happily with his wife Virginia, and they enjoy the grandchildren they are blessed with from their five children: Elia, Manuel, Pedro, Rafael, and Gabriel—all believers in the same Adventist faith.

What does science say about the power of religion?

A number of studies have shown that those who practice a religion or who say that religion is important in their lives enjoy better health and live longer even if they suffer with a chronic disease.[1] Those who are religious are more likely to lead a healthy life, says researcher Sonja Lyubomirsky.[2] They also have the ability to better withstand a loss (e.g., the death of a child) than those who are not religious.[3] Religious folks smoke and drink less than nonreligious folks, and some, like Seventh-day Adventists, recommend a healthy lifestyle: good nutrition; abstinence from alcohol, drugs, and tobacco; and a positive attitude, with their conscience at peace and consequently a lower stress level. Adventists who follow these guidelines, on average, live longer and better than the population in general.[4] It was also found that 47 percent of those who attend religious services several times a week describe themselves as "very happy," compared with 28 percent who attend less than once per month.[5] Other research has confirmed that religious, or spiritual, people are happier than atheists or agnostics: they have better mental health and cope better with stress, their marriages are more successful, they use less drugs and alcohol, they are physically healthier, and they live longer.[6] Of course, an atheist can be very spiritual, and someone who says he is a believer can for all practical purposes be an atheist. What we are talking about here are people who are committed to their faith.

A considerable number of studies confirm these findings, in which religious folks show a lower degree of depression, have better physical health, smoke less, have more social support, and even have dwellings that are more comfortable.[7] This is seen not only among Christians but also other religious communities. These positive results for health, welfare, and happiness are also found among Muslim believers and Hindu populations.[8]

Jesus and faith

Probably after becoming an adolescent, a certain young lady noticed that something was not right in her body. Her menstrual periods were very long, and the bleeding never seemed to cease. At first her mother did not take it very seriously. "It'll soon become regular," she said reassuringly. But that didn't turn out to be the case; the girl's bleeding barely stopped before the cycle began again. The continued bleeding was detrimental to her healthy development; she was skinny, almost emaciated. The chauvinist society she lived in had very strict moral beliefs; it considered female menstruation a state of impurity and believed that women on their menstrual cycle should be kept isolated to avoid contaminating the men and the things they touched. This made her suffering even worse. She sought help, but nothing and nobody could do anything for her. She lived under a shadow of concern and shame, locking herself away in her room to avoid the gossip and indiscretions of people who might see her.

Years passed and the problem persisted. The stigma, humiliation, and withdrawal intensified her negative self-worth. She was further weakened by the thought of never finding a cure. The sad reality was that there was no remedy for chronic menorrhagia, probably the result of some genetic pelvic malformation. Nevertheless, the woman spoken of in this story in Matthew 9:20–22, with the passing years and in her lonely suffering, clung tenaciously to hope and belief in a divine solution. Perhaps at some point she began to find comfort in prayer, always desirous that God would grant her a miracle. Reading the Bible stories of how God had worked in the past through His prophets and holy servants to heal lepers and people with other diseases confirmed in her the notion that she, too, could be similarly blessed. Thus conviction and faith were strengthened and hope increased. It was then that she began to hear of Jesus of Nazareth.

Many had seen Him perform miracles, and there were amazing stories circulating about extraordinary healings. As she heard more about His teachings and works, she became convinced that He was a messenger of God and the great hope for her personal need. The problem was that the Rabbi did not stay in a specific place but continually traveled, especially in the regions of Judea and in Jerusalem. She lived in a town of Galilee, on the shores of Lake Gennesaret.

The Master and His disciples had been in several places in Galilee, but she did not know whether He would ever pass through her town. Then, one day she received the most thrilling news of her life: "Jesus and His disciples are returning from Gadara and will pass through our town."

This was her great opportunity. With considerable effort, she dressed and went out into the streets. Barely able to shuffle along because of her chronic weakness, at last she caught a glimpse of a crowd coming her way, and in its midst was the Divine Healer along with His disciples. But how could she ever get near Jesus with so many people crowding in close to Him? It was practically impossible! Then she saw that the multitude was coming straight down the street in her direction, and she felt a sensation that God was acting in her behalf in answer to her prayers. She tried to position herself where He would pass, but there were many noisy people coming, and it was going to be hard to get close enough to speak to Him or be heard. Her strength was at its limit, and the shoving was more than she could withstand; somebody bumped her unawares, and she fell to the ground. Jesus was now within arm's length, so she reached out toward His passing figure. The thought flashed through her mind: *If I can only touch the hem of His garment, something wonderful will happen!* So placing all her strength in that last effort, she stretched out her hand until she touched the Master's garment. Then the miracle occurred. She instantly knew deep inside that she was healed, and it felt more wonderful than words could describe! There was perfect comfort where a moment before the ever-present pain had held her in its grip. She sat there reveling in gratitude and joy. Now the crowd had stopped, and Jesus turned and extended His hand to her and helped her to her feet. That hand was an invitation to the beginning of a new life with a promise of fulfillment and happiness for all her future years. Jesus had given life to her dreams.

Why and how to practice faith

Considering the multiple benefits provided by the exercise of religious activities and the cultivation of spirituality, especially raising levels of personal happiness, various researchers now suggest that people attend church and spend time in meditation or reading devotional books. For example, the Russian researcher Sonja Lyubomirsky, an expert on the subject, proposes in her book, *The How of Happiness: A Scientific Approach to Getting the Life You Want*, the following activities that have been confirmed by empirical evidence to help you feel better and enjoy improved health:

1. Join a church; take part in spiritual programs or in a group Bible study.
2. Attend a religious service once a week or more often.
3. Spend at least fifteen minutes a day reading the Bible or a religious book, or listen to a religious broadcast on the radio or on television.
4. Volunteer to do charity work with a faith-based organization.
5. Look for the meaning of life. Work to find a faith with which you can relate.
6. Spend between five minutes to one hour per day in prayer (pray when you awake, pray at every meal, and pray again when you go to bed).
7. Develop your ability to see the sacred in everyday things, both in the beautiful and in the simple. "Sanctifying day-to-day objects, experiences and struggles takes a great deal of practice, but it's at the heart of spirituality and its rewards."[9]

Bible Teaching: Jesus and Faith
(Matthew 9:18–22)

Introduction
One Sunday, a minister was talking about baptism and said it was enough just to sprinkle water over the heads of the believers to baptize them. He explained that when John the Baptist baptized Jesus in the Jordan, in reality they were not in the water but close by on the banks of the river. And the same thing happened when Philip baptized the eunuch by the river. At the close of the religious service, a believer approached him and said, "Now I understand the story of Jonah, who was swallowed by the whale. That always worried me. Now I know that Jonah was not really inside the whale but close by, over to one side. Same thing with the three Hebrew youths cast into the fiery furnace . . . not really inside, just over to the side. And of course there was Daniel who wasn't actually thrown into the lions' den but was placed to one side, like at the zoo."

Previously, we talked about death and resurrection. In this study we will see how death and spiritual resurrection are symbolized.

Let's consider what the Bible says about baptism, which is the entrance to a new life and sanctification; in other words, the entry into the practice of religion:

Why did death come into this world? *(Romans 5:12)*
God created man in His image and likeness, perfect, and with the possibility of living forever. But eternity was conditional upon obedience. When Adam sinned, death came into this world.

What did God do with humankind after the Fall? *(Genesis 3:15)*
Despite Adam's disobedience, God promised to provide a solution to the sin problem: He would send a Savior born of a woman. Born among men, yet as eternal as the offended law, Jesus was as human as Adam the offender. Because a man (Adam) had been the cause of the fall of this world, only another Man (Jesus) could restore it.

What did Jesus do to restore this lost world? *(Romans 5:6–11)*
Jesus' death was sufficient to save us, because He lived His life in complete obedience to the will of His Father as expressed in His law. In His obedience, He obtained eternity. In order to bestow on us eternal life, God today de-

mands the same of us as He did in Eden: obedience to His law. Because we cannot perfectly obey the law, Jesus did that for us so that we, by His obedience, can be made righteous and thus attain eternity.

How can I accept Jesus, receive His righteousness, and be cleansed of my sins and be reconciled with God? *(Acts 22:16)*

When we accept Jesus, we agree to receive His righteousness, and through faith in Him we are cleansed of our sins. But that faith always produces fruit: repentance, followed by confession and a changed life. Genuine conversion is expressed in genuine works of faith (James 2:26; 1 Thessalonians 1:3). When we accept Jesus as our personal Savior, He reconciles us with God.

What religious practice represents our surrender to Jesus and acceptance of His life and death? *(Romans 6:3–5)*

Baptism by immersion is the religious act whereby we publicly confess belief in Jesus as our personal Savior. In turn, it represents the beginning of our new life in Him. It is the testimony of a life that was justified (past event) and will be sanctified (present and on into the future) through practicing faith, which is, literally, the healthy practice of religion.

What did Jesus say about baptism? *(John 3:3–5)*

Jesus compared baptism with the new birth. Being born of the Spirit is to accept Him into our hearts. And to be born of the water is our public confession of acceptance through baptism. Some might say, "I'm not ready for this," but in reality no one is ready to be born. Spiritual rebirth does not come from man but from God. When we accept Jesus sincerely, we are born again. Without this birth, there can be no superior life.

Is baptism indispensable to our walking with God? *(Mark 16:16)*

These are direct words from Jesus. If you believe in Jesus, fear not. Advance along the path of salvation.

Conclusion

True faith leads me to live a true religion. The word *religion* comes from the Latin expression *religare*, which means: *re*, to return; *ligare*, to unite—that is, reuniting man with God. Only in Him are we complete. Only if we accept Jesus, obey His Word, and put into practice His counsels will we have fullness of life. For this reason, accept Christ today and be born into His kingdom of grace. To have a tomorrow, you need to be reborn today. Erich Sauer has said: "No man can follow Christ and yet be lost."

An appeal
Will you be baptized as a public expression of your acceptance of Jesus as your personal Savior?

My resolve

I accept the grace of God and His righteousness, and I will be baptized to unite myself with Christ.

I sign this in acceptance: _____.

How Religious Am I?
Evaluation of My Religious Life

The list presented below contains a series of statements. Read each and place an *X* in the box that best describes your thoughts on the content of those statements.

	Statements	Always	Often	Sometimes	Rarely	Never	Score
1	My faith encompasses all aspects of my life.						
2	I have had the experience of feeling the presence of God.						
3	I believe that we should seek God's help when we have to make important decisions.						
4	My faith incapacitates me to act as I want.						
5	The most important thing for me is to serve God as best I can.						
6	I try to apply my religion to all aspects of my life.						
7	I think there are more important things in life than religion.						
8	I believe that the main thing in a religious belief system is to practice a morally correct life.						
9	I am opposed to religious ideas influencing my way of life.						
10	My religious principles are the foundation of my view of life.						
						TOTAL	

Interpretation for the evaluation of my religious life

1. For questions 1, 2, 3, 5, 6, 8, and 10, assign the following score: always = 5; often = 4; sometimes = 3; rarely = 2; and never = 1.
2. For questions 4, 7, and 9, assign the following score: always = 1; often = 2; sometimes = 3; rarely = 4; and never = 5.
3. Add up the points of the ten questions and then look at the following interpretation.

Results

Between 47 and 50 points ....Excellent religious life

Between 42 and 46 points ....Very good religious life

Between 35 and 41 points ....Average religious life

Between 30 and 34 points .... Poor religious life

Fewer than 30 points .... Very poor religious life

---

1. Douglas Oman and Dwayne Reed, "Religion and Mortality Among the Community-Dwelling Elderly," *American Journal of Public Health* 88, no. 10 (October 1998): 1469–1475, doi: 10.2105/AJPH.88.10.1469.

2. Lyubomirsky, *The How of Happiness* (see chap. 4, n. 1).

3. Daniel N. McIntosh, Roxane Cohen Silver, and Camille B. Wortman, "Religion's Role in Adjustment to a Negative Life Event: Coping With the Loss of a Child," *Journal of Personality and Social Psychology* 65, no. 4 (October 1993): 812–821, doi: 10.1037/0022-3514.65.4.812.

4. Harold Koenig et al., "Modeling the Cross-Sectional Relationships Between Religion, Physical Health, Social Support, and Depressive Symptoms," *American Journal of Geriatric Psychiatry* 5, no. 2 (February 1997): 131–144, doi: 10.1097/00019442-199721520-00006.

5. David G. Myers, "The Funds, Friends, and Faith of Happy People," *American Psychologist* 55, no. 1 (January 2000): 56–67, doi: 10.1037/0003-066X.55.1.56.

6. Srinivasan Chokkanathan, "Religiosity and Well-Being of Older Adults in Chennai, India," *Aging and Mental Health* 17, no. 7 (April 2013): 880–887, doi: 10.1080/13607863.2013.790924.

7. Kenneth I. Pargament and Annette Mahoney, "Spirituality: Discovering and Conserving the Sacred," in *Handbook of Positive Psychology*, eds. C. R. Snyder and Shane J. López (New York: Oxford University Press, 2002), 646–659; Abebaw Yohannes et al., "Health Behaviour, Depression and Religiosity in Older Patients Admitted to Intermediate Care," *International Journal of Geriatric Psychiatry* 23, no. 7 (July 2008): 735–740.

8. Ahmed Abdel-Khalek, "The Relationships Between Subjective Well-Being, Health, and Religiosity Among Young Adults From Qatar," *Mental Health, Religion & Culture* 16, no. 3 (2013): 306–318.

9. Lyubomirsky, *The How of Happiness*, 233–239.

Chapter 8

The Blessed Hope

Surely I come quickly.
—Revelation 22:20, KJV

That morning, Carlos came home drunk. In the darkness of the living room, his wife, Constanza, was waiting for him on the couch. She had been there for hours, sometimes dozing and then struggling with herself to stay awake. She wanted to see her husband when he got home . . . the home she had worked so hard and with such great hopes to make into a lovely nest for them. But now it seemed to be falling apart. She wanted to look her husband in the eyes; but in her pain she didn't really know what she would say. Her heart had been repeatedly broken.

When Carlos opened the front door, he saw his wife in the semidarkness of the room, and the only thing his clouded mind could come up with was an incongruous question: "Do you love me?" Carlos didn't wait for an answer. He went to bed.

Constanza awoke later that morning in tears, confused and still on the couch. It was Sabbath, and she was an Adventist believer. So she went to church and laid out her uncertainty before the pastor, who after listening understandingly, gave her this wise advice: "Go home and embrace your husband."

Constanza returned home that morning and with more uncertainty in her mind than in her heart, she embraced Carlos. The embrace lasted as long as it took for her husband to finally wake up.

When Carlos opened his eyes, he felt the warm embrace of the one who loved him despite everything. Until then he had understood nothing about love. There was his wife, loving him dearly and following the biblical counsel given to believing wives: "So that, if any of them do not believe the word, they may be won over without words by the behavior of their wives" (1 Peter 3:1, NIV).

That morning Carlos began to understand that love does not bestow what one deserves but what one needs. And deep in his being he recognized the superiority of his wife's love. Carlos had experienced Constanza's love many times, but that morning he finally "woke up." She exuded such warm tenderness that the sharp edges of his heart were softened, turning everything into a delightful promise. He had denied, many times, these pleasures. But lately he was like a wanderer out in a freezing blizzard, seeking the gaze of his wife to return him to the green leaves of springtime and the beauty of summer sunsets. Constanza did not refuse his eyes that gaze. This is the power of a woman who loves, and the philosopher Friedrich Nietzsche sensed that when he wrote, "The perfect woman is a higher type of human than the perfect man."

Like piercing light, Constanza's love flooded Carlos's heart with natural ease. Love flows effortlessly once the will steps forward to open the floodgates of the heart. Light, irresistible for the simple fact of being light, illuminates all things; likewise, irresistible love was kindled in Carlos's heart. Love, like beauty, has this quality; it is superior to intelligence, it needs no explanation. It is beyond all understanding because it comes from God. "God is love" (1 John 4:8).

Drunkenness and violence masked Carlos's fear of being left out in the darkness of life. But now, hand in hand with Constanza, he began to draw near to God and to attend church with his wife.

One Sabbath morning, a preacher said something that changed the course of Carlos's life: "Those persons who were abused in childhood often become abusers as adults." After hearing those words, Carlos began to bring back from hidden recesses of his mind the memory of being sexually abused when he was six years old. Those comments from that sermon opened before him a difficult and painful path but one that in time would help him find himself, and find restorative peace.

From that moment, Carlos felt that God was leading him into a desert experience as He had done with Jesus. He trusted, nevertheless, that he would not be alone, because Jesus had already gone through that for humankind so that no one should have to experience such solitude in this world ever again.

Carlos began studying the Bible with an Adventist pastor and learned that God does not lead anyone into the desert only to be left abandoned. He guides His followers through the desert and on to the Promised Land, as in the story of the people of Israel in ancient times. For Carlos, the Promised Land was a new life here and now, a new way of seeing himself and a power to overcome depression and his inner violence that on a couple of occasions almost led him to the grave. Carlos still carries on his body the scar from a bullet that God did not allow to take his life. Having seen the miracle, Carlos embraced the hope of Christ's second coming and was baptized into the Adventist faith on Saturday, May 5, 2007, in Cuba. This "blessed hope" (Titus 2:13) gave wonderful new meaning to his life.

Life was not easy for Carlos after conversion and baptism. Life is never easy for one who was abused of his innocence as a child. It is not easy for a man who bears a burden of undeserved guilt. It is hard, like an ember drawn from the fire trying to preserve its glow and heat. Life is not easy. Life is full of injustice, full of things we do not understand or deserve, things not anticipated or expected. But Carlos was learning not to blame God.

It's nine at night in the city of Boise, Idaho, where I sit writing these lines while I communicate with Carlos via Skype:

"What does the promise of the second coming of Christ mean to your life?" I ask.

Carlos takes his time before responding: "Nobody has ever asked me that question before. What comes to mind are the words of Paul: 'Eye hath not seen, nor ear heard, neither have entered into the heart of man, the things which God hath prepared for them that love him' [1 Corinthians 2:9, KJV]. Many of those promised things I have already received in this life. Jesus has become everything to me. I can do nothing alone, but the infinite grace of God performs miracles in me every day. I think the second coming of Christ will mean coming face-to-face with the Friend who accompanied me on the path of life even before I knew He was there beside me."

Ready to take my leave, I asked Carlos to summarize his faith briefly for me.

"I think that my healing was a long, difficult, and miraculous process. God was at work in me before I even knew Him. He did it quietly but effectively. At first, I was very angry with Him because He did not protect me in my childhood. Then I realized that evil does not come from Him, that evil is the consequence of sin. And I realized that God is a God of second chances. He always gives me what I need; not what I deserve. His grace is infinite. When my past begins to torment me, I look to Jesus and His words: 'Let not your heart be troubled. You believe in God. Believe also in Me. In my Father's house are many dwelling places. . . . And if I go and prepare a place for you, I will come again and receive you to Myself, that where I am, you may be also' " (John 14:1–3, MEV).

Today, Carlos and Constanza are a pastoral couple. His ministry inspires the lives of thousands of people. Sharing faith is everything for them. Within a few days, Carlos will talk to the person who abused him as a child, in order to have closure to a sad chapter of his life and to share with his attacker the hope of Christ's second coming, which has given meaning to his existence and which every day lights a sacred flame in his heart.

What does science say about hope?

Every year about three thousand scientific papers are released based on research related to the impact of hope on mental health. But all of this is written from a humanistic perspective and concerns what is called immanent hope, which has nothing to do with transcendent hope, such as that expressed in the Word of God. There are very few studies focused on the transcendent hope looking to the second coming of Christ. The only test that evaluates hope in a "world of joy that is beyond" is the TED-R (see the evaluation at the end of the chapter). With this instrument some interesting results have been obtained. In a sample of 176 married adults, about thirty-nine years old on average, it was found that those with the highest transcendent hope had higher marital satisfaction and were less likely to divorce.[1] These results were corroborated in other recent research.[2]

In another study of 230 people, it was found that those who believed in the second coming of Christ did not suffer as much from depression.[3] An investigation conducted with 175 college students found that those who had high levels of transcendent hope had significantly fewer symptoms of anxiety, paranoia, somatization, obsessions, hostility, and psychological toxicity and in general had much better mental health.[4] Similar results were found in a previous study with a sample of 350 adolescents and young people.[5]

Perhaps the most significant study is that conducted by Alcantara,[6] with 208 elderly people, which investigated the relationship between transcendent hope and quality of life, according to the concept of the World Health Organization (WHO). Those who expressed a belief in the second coming of Christ revealed the highest levels of quality of life in physical, social, mental, and spiritual categories. Another significant piece of data shown in all the comparative studies is that believers in the Second Advent reported higher levels of transcendent hope than other groups of believers or nonbelievers.[7]

In summary, one can say that there is empirical evidence to demonstrate that those who embrace faith in the second coming of Christ have better physical and mental health, feel better about themselves and others, and especially have better marriages and families.

The apostle Paul says, "The grace of God that brings salvation has appeared to all men, teaching us that, denying ungodliness and worldly lusts, we should live soberly, righteously and godly in the present age, looking for the blessed hope and glorious appearing of our great God and Savior Jesus Christ" (Titus 2:11–13, NKJV).

At the end of His ministry, the Lord Jesus Christ gathered His disciples for a farewell meeting. He informed them that it was time for Him to return to the Father and that they would not see Him anymore. That news, although expected, was like the lash of a whip to the soul. A wrenching sensation invaded them, filling them with anguish and helplessness. For more than three years the disciples had largely abandoned their families, their work, and everything else that previously constituted their daily routine, in order to follow the Master all around Palestine. They had heard the voice of Jesus, accepted His call, and received His blessings. They were happy with the Master, cherishing the vision of establishing a kingdom of love on Earth. But now He was telling them that it was all over, the light of hope was going out. Yet amid the grief and loneliness, the Master lit up their hearts again with a wonderful promise—the glorious hope of a transcendent future, without separation, in the house of His Father: "Do not let your hearts be troubled. You believe in God; believe also in me. My Father's house has many rooms; if that were not so, would I have told you that I am going there to prepare a place for you? And if I go and prepare a place for you, I will come back and take you to be with me that you also may be where I am" (John 14:1–3, NIV).

The promise of Jesus' personal return was foundational to the hope of the early disciples, to the whole community of believers throughout history, and one of the recurring themes of biblical writings. This is reconfirmed during the ascension of Jesus; the book of Acts tells us that the disciples were watching the event, "when suddenly two men dressed in white robes stood beside them. 'Men of Galilee,' they said, 'why do you stand here looking into the sky? This same Jesus, who has been taken from you into heaven, will come back in the same way you have seen him go into heaven" (Acts 1:10, 11, NIV).

This *transcendent* hope is the epicenter of all Christian theology. It clarifies the nature and state of the dead because those who have died with that hope will be raised to life at the return of the Lord.

Obviously, if the soul was immortal, if man passed to the "great beyond" without experiencing death, the return of Christ and the resurrection would make no sense. It would suffice to move directly to God's judgment once a person's body perishes: assigned to heaven or hell. But hope in the second coming of Christ tells us that man is mortal, and therefore it is necessary for the Son of God to return to Earth to complete His redemptive work. At that time His mission is not to free us from the power of sin but to free us from the presence of evil.

The issue of death is a very serious one. Faith does not reduce the weight of that matter; presumption, on the other hand, might claim otherwise. It is easy to think that by chanting a few "Our Fathers" and doing some good works on Earth we can buy some real estate in heaven. But that by no means is the case. Death brings to a close all of man's senses in this world. Unless we comprehend seriously what death is, we cannot appreciate the value of faith that sees beyond this world; and we cannot appreciate Christ or the promise of His second coming or the true value of life in all its magnitude.

To understand the meaning of the second coming of Christ, let's consider again what we saw in the Bible study on pages 87 and 88. The Bible says that God "formed man of the dust of the ground, and breathed into his nostrils the breath of life; and man became a living being" (Genesis 2:7, NKJV). So, we come from the earth. In a more literary sense, we can say that we are "star dust," made from the matter of the universe. It sounds poetic. But we are, to be sure, no more than a blend of dust and time. Our genealogy begins and ends on the earth, and that is our humbling reality.

The Hebrew term in Genesis 2:7 translated as "living being" or "living soul" is *nephesh chayyah*. This designates not only man but also marine animals, insects, reptiles, and beasts—all living things (Genesis 1:20, 24; 2:19). Scripture says that man became "a living being" (Genesis 2:7, NKJV). Nothing in the Creation story indicates that man received a soul; that is, some kind of separate entity joined to the human body when he was created.

The Hebrew word *nephesh*, translated "soul," denotes individuality or personality; meanwhile, the Old Testament Hebrew word *ruach*, translated "spirit," refers to the spark of life essential for human existence. It describes the divine energy or vital principle that animates human beings and all living things. Psalm 146:4 says that when a person dies, the breath (*ruach*) leaves the body. "The dust returns to the earth as it was: and the spirit [*ruach*] returns to God who gave it" (Ecclesiastes 12:7, ESV; cf. Job 34:14). In the Bible, neither *nephesh* nor *ruach* denote an intelligent entity separate from the physical body. Therefore, when a human being dies, he or she quite simply dies. He or she goes nowhere.

Paul exclaims triumphantly: "Death is swallowed up in victory. O Death, where is your sting? O Hades, where is your victory?" (1 Corinthians 15:54, 55, NKJV). This is the hope of the believer who is not born of this earth but is born of heaven.

This is how the apostle Paul explains it:

> Brothers and sisters, we do not want you to be uninformed about those who sleep in death, so that you do not grieve like the rest of mankind, who have no hope. For we believe that Jesus died and rose again, and so we believe that God will bring with Jesus those who have fallen asleep

in him. According to the Lord's word, we tell you that we who are still alive, who are left until the coming of the Lord, will certainly not precede those who have fallen asleep. For the Lord himself will come down from heaven, with a loud command, with the voice of the archangel and with the trumpet call of God, and the dead in Christ will rise first. After that, we who are still alive and are left will be caught up together with them in the clouds to meet the Lord in the air. And so we will be with the Lord forever (1 Thessalonians 4:13–17, NIV; see also 1 Corinthians 15:51–55; Malachi 4:1–3; 2 Peter 3:10–13).

In other words, there is no heaven or hell or purgatory after you die. There is rest. But while we are alive, there is hope of the resurrection at the second coming of Jesus. Therefore, the members of the early Christian community greeted each other with the expression *Maranatha*, "the Lord is coming," which for them became a victory cry in the face of persecution and death and a song of life restored.

Even the rite of the Lord's Supper is understood from the perspective of transcendent hope. Paul again says: "For I received from the Lord what I also passed on to you: The Lord Jesus, on the night he was betrayed, took bread, and when he had given thanks, he broke it and said, 'This is my body, which is for you; do this in remembrance of me.' In the same way, after supper he took the cup, saying, 'This cup is the new covenant in my blood; do this, whenever you drink it, in remembrance of me.' For whenever you eat this bread and drink this cup, you proclaim the Lord's death until he comes" (1 Corinthians 11:23–26, NIV).

Consequently, by partaking of the sacred emblems of the eucharistic banquet, the Christian no longer participates merely in nostalgic remembrance or in repeated honor of a bygone event but proclaims the future unfolding of redemption's promises. These reenactments of the Communion service rescue the past from the darkness of death and project our hope forward to life's bright future. The rite is not limited to archaeology of the past or a chronicle of history; it rides on the back of prophecy to open up a future of promise guaranteed by God. The Cross is absorbed in hope. The open tomb in that Judean hillside now proclaims the day when all of Earth's cemeteries will give up their dead at last. These will rise victoriously in Christ to eternal life.

It is for this reason that we call this spiritual truth the "blessed hope" (Titus 2:13), it secures the soul like a steadfast anchor (see Hebrews 6:17–20); it is like a "fortress" (Psalm 91:2) or a "stronghold" (Zechariah 9:12) that protects us from the discouragements that assail us. It also secures and fortifies faith in God, who is our hope (see Psalm 71:5). It illuminates the horizons of the future with promises and lifts us on wings above distress or unhappiness (see Hosea 2:14, 15). It is the hope of a "new world" where "there will be no more death or mourning or crying or pain" (Revelation 21:4, NIV) because all things will be made new (see verses 1–5).

How can we take hold of and cultivate this hope?

Just a few weeks ago I met a young Adventist couple in Miami, Florida, during an evangelistic series that I conducted in their home church. Following the Thursday evening presentation, Ailen and Jorge invited me to dinner. They wanted to meet me and share their story. I gladly accepted: There is always a story worth hearing when it comes to Cuban immigrants.

After dinner, we enjoyed a very pleasant conversation under the light of an autumn moon. It was truly a serene evening for conversing. Ailen and Jorge are young people not yet to middle age, if indeed life can be halved at some middle point; life seems more naturally divided and classified by memories than simply by passing years. We live life in the present and take it as it comes. And these young Cubans learned to live that way, without asking for explanations or wallowing in complaints.

Cubans and Uruguayans come up with the most bizarre combinations to name their children: From Washington Pérez to Leira González, which is nothing other than Ariel spelled backward. (The most original Cuban name I have come across is Usnavy, for US Navy.) There is always a story behind our names, so I asked Ailen to tell me about her early life and the name she had been given.

"My father, Martín Zaceta, took the name of my mother, Nelia, and inverted it, thus, Ailen. I think my birth determined my character: Ever since my mother told me the details of my birth, I have learned to live with gratitude. My life is a miracle, as is the life of every newborn babe. I was born in the Workers' Maternity Hospital in Havana, on a sweltering evening on March 8, 1976. Nothing unusual, other than my mother choosing the wrong place to give birth. The hospital was under reconstruction, and the doctors barely had time to improvise a surgery room in one of the corridors of the hospital. My birth was complicated, and my mother thought it was all over when the doctor whispered into her ear: "Do you have other children?" Mother prayed for me, not for her own life. And finally she gave birth to me, utterly exhausted and in great pain. The doctor was amazed that the two of us came out alive following the severe trauma we had gone through."

Jorge looked tenderly at his dear wife, while twirling a lock of her jet-black hair around his finger. Perhaps he was thinking of his own origins and the miracle of eventually finding this enchanting companion as his wife. The union of two people always hides a mystery.

"What other things determined your faith and destiny?" I asked Ailen.

"Constant shortage. There is a saying that goes: 'One who hasn't suffered shortage doesn't store up for later.' "

I asked—not without some irony—whether that was a Cuban saying, for they certainly know how it is to deal with poverty. She countered, "No," in the same tone and we laughed. But it is true, as the Greek philosopher Epicurus said, a man is rich if he gets to know shortage first. This young couple possessed richness.

"My father," continued Ailen, "was a farmer who taught me many things from simple observation of nature. He can discern exactly what to plant and at what time of the day. He has a special way of coaxing from the earth its fruits. He seems to sniff that from the humidity in the air. My father taught me to wait patiently for the right time when making decisions. He taught me to interpret the times, because as wise Solomon said, 'There's a season for everything, and a time for every matter under the heavens, a time to for giving birth and a time for dying; a time for planting and a time for uprooting what was planted' " (Ecclesiastes 3:1, 2, CEB).

"And your time, Jorge? What was your time?" I asked.

"There is a hinge in my time. It was on August 17, 2010. On that day I sealed my covenant with God in the waters of the Atlantic Ocean, more precisely at Miami Beach, close to where we are now living. Baptism was the most important moment of my spiritual life. There is deep meaning in the words of Jesus to Nicodemus: 'Unless a man is born of water and the Spirit, he cannot enter the kingdom of God' [John 3:5, MEV]. That birth was the result of a long process that began in the early years of my life of ups and downs in my tug-of-war with God."

"Why was baptism important for you?"

"Because baptism is a death but also a resurrection. The human being is a zombie, a dead man walking. We're all dead but still breathing. Baptism tells us that life consists not just of the mechanical act of breathing but of being in God and in Christ, the divine vehicle of life. Paul explains it this way: 'Do you not know that all of us who have been baptized into Christ Jesus were baptized into his death? We were buried therefore with him by baptism into death, so that as Christ was raised from the dead by the glory of the Father, we too might walk in newness of life' [Romans 6:3, 4, RSV]. This is the new life that leads us into the kingdom of God. And I believe that this covenant with God opened up a new horizon for me when I was looking for a wife of my own faith. Everything has changed for me since August 17, 2010."

Our conversation was becoming more interesting, and time had flown by.

The waiter passed by the table to ask whether we needed anything more. That was a subtle suggestion that, if not, perhaps we could move along because they wanted to close the restaurant. We continued the conversation on the way to the hotel where I was staying.

"How do you await the coming of Christ? There are believers who become paranoid and are so focused on the timing of the Second Advent that they forget to practice their faith."

Ailen spoke up: "Our common faith brought Jorge and I together, and from the time we were married four years ago, we have wondered what meaning lies behind our forming a family and how we can build bridges to reach others. Chapter 25 of Matthew helped us understand the meaning of our faith. The entire chapter speaks of the meaning of life as we await the kingdom. Those who are finally saved are out there doing something for their fellow man. True religion is not about what you believe but about what you do with what you say you believe. It isn't the beliefs that make us better people but what we do in behalf of others. We need to bear the yoke with others.

"My father taught me lessons from observing the oxen he had in Cuba. From him I learned the key to not feeling overly burdened when committed to helping others face their struggles and pain. A good pair of oxen is composed of a weaker or younger one and an older or stronger ox. The way in which the yoke is set up—with its adjustments of iron, wood, or leather— tells you which ox is pulling the main part of the burden. Jesus used the figure of the yoke to refer to the load that He is willing to bear. He always carries the heaviest weight, because He is the strongest. That is why Jesus said, 'Take up my yoke upon you, and learn from me, for I am meek and humble in heart; and ye shall find rest to your souls; for my yoke is easy, and my burden is light' " (Matthew 11:29, 30, YLT).

* * * * *

Jorge and Ailen were married on May 20, 2011. They have two children, Michael, four, and Victoria, one year old. They make a beautiful couple of Adventist believers. They manage the Angels on Earth Foundation in Miami, which is dedicated to raising funds to help children whose parents do not have the economic capacity to meet their medical costs.

The idea for the foundation came when Reivys Zaceta, a nurse at Holtz Children's Hospital in Miami, referred an urgent case to his sister Ailen. A little girl named Monica, from Saltillo, Coahuila, a small town in Mexico, was born with short bowel syndrome. Actually, Monica's struggle for survival had begun even before birth. When the mother learned that her daughter would be born with a deformity, she wanted to abort, but the father objected. The mother finally ended up leaving her family, and baby Monica went to several hospitals in Mexico, where nobody seemed willing to do anything for her except for one kindhearted physician. That doctor told the child's father, Enrique Hernandez, about one of the few hospitals in the world attending cases like Monica's. Enrique asked for a humanitarian visa, and within forty-eight hours of the last hospitalization of his daughter, he traveled from Mexico City to Miami. As he sat with his little daughter on the plane, a series of "coincidences" began to occur. First, Enrique asked God to help him administer medication to his daughter. He felt incapable of doing it correctly. As soon as he finished praying about that a lovely young nurse sat down beside him and offered to take charge! During the flight, there was a man seated behind Enrique, and he overheard the drama of what the father and little one were going through. The fellow passenger offered Enrique a considerable sum of money to help fund the hospital expenses. But even so, that money was not enough to cover the million dollars it would cost for Monica's surgery and related costs. Within a few weeks of this, Reivys referred the case to Ailen, and together they founded the Angels on Earth Foundation to help children in need like little Monica.

Today, Enrique Hernandez is a believer encouraged by the blessed hope of the coming of Christ. Monica continues in her recovery. Both father and daughter are grateful to Jorge and Ailen because they live their faith with good works (1 Thessalonians 1:3).

Bible Teaching: Jesus and the Blessed Hope
(John 14:1–3)

Introduction

When the Trojan War came to an end, Ulysses wanted to return to Ithaca, his beloved land, but many mishaps delayed the homeward journey. Meanwhile, his wife Penelope longingly awaited his return. Pestered and courted by many men who insisted that Ulysses must surely be dead, Penelope refused to believe that. She remained steadfastly loyal to her marriage vows. At last the day came and Ulysses returned and took his unwavering wife into his arms.

Jesus was about to go to His death, but He was confident that afterward He would return to the bosom of His Father. He knew that His disciples would be saddened by His absence, so He gladdened their hearts with "the blessed hope" of His return someday to gather them up to be with Him forever. But was that promise only for His disciples? Who else was given this promise? And when will it be fulfilled?

Let us review what the Bible says about the second coming of Christ:

Was the promise of Jesus' second coming only for His disciples? *(Matthew 24:30)*

All the nations of the world will take pleasure in the most extraordinary event in the history of the universe. Jesus will return with power and great glory.

What will happen when He returns? *(Matthew 24:31; 2 Peter 3:10)*

On that glorious day Jesus will come with His angels. He will gather His elect from one end of the earth to the other. The planet will be shaken to its foundations as never before, and it will be consumed with fire.

What other things will happen at that time? *(1 Corinthians 15:51–55)*

On that day the dead will be raised to immortality, and those who are alive will be transformed in "the twinkling of an eye."

Can we know when this great event will happen? *(Matthew 24:36)*

The Lord Jesus was clear when He said that no man knows the day and time of His return.

What did Jesus say would happen before His return to this world? *(Matthew 24:3–14)*

The events described by Jesus as signs of His return are dramatically being fulfilled today before our eyes. Just turn on your television and watch the news to see how everything is being fulfilled to the letter.

If all the signs described by Jesus are being met with pinpoint accuracy, why has He not yet come? *(2 Peter 3:9)*

The Lord has not yet returned because He is waiting for you to accept His loving embrace. Today is the day to give yourself to Him and prepare for His coming.

How does the Bible conclude? *(Revelation 22:20)*

Jesus promised, "Surely I come quickly."

Conclusion

Revelation 22:17 says, "The Spirit and the bride say, Come. And let him that heareth say, Come. And let him that is athirst come. And whosoever will, let him take the water of life freely." The question is posed: "Why live in this unstable world if we can live in Paradise with God?"

An appeal

Will you accept the grace of Jesus and prepare to meet Him?

My resolve

I accept the saving grace of Jesus and am willing to study His Word every day to prepare for His coming and also to help others be prepared.

I sign this in acceptance: _____.

How Hopeful Am I?
Evaluation of Hope

Based on the Hope-Hopelessness-Revised (TED-R) test by Mario Pereyra (2013)

	Statements	Always	Often	Sometimes	Rarely	Never	Score
1	Instead of crushing me, adversity and problems encourage me to keep fighting.						
2	I think people are so false that nobody can be trusted.						
3	I believe that with God's help, it is possible to achieve what one proposes.						
4	I recall past experiences that have left me so affected that I'll probably never get over them.						
5	I believe God's promise that there is a happy world beyond this earthly life.						
6	Over the years, I have had experiences over which I had no control.						
7	I am attracted to new projects and the possibility of creating different things.						
8	I see a very dark panorama in my life.						
9	I enjoy every day and want to live as much as possible.						

10	Bad luck follows me, and I have the feeling that things will continue going bad.							
11	I believe that something good can come of the worst tragedy.							
12	I get discouraged and depressed easily.							
13	I look toward tomorrow, placing my trust in God.							
14	I have thoughts of ending my life.							
15	I feel that I still have important things to accomplish in life.							
16	I do not believe that God exists or that there is something else after death.							
							TOTAL	

Interpretation for the TED-R Test

1. For questions 1, 3, 5, 7, 9, 11, 13, and 15, assign the following score: always = 5; often = 4; sometimes = 3; rarely = 2; and never = 1.

2. For questions 2, 4, 6, 8, 10, 12, 14, and 16, assign the following score: always = 1; often = 2; sometimes = 3; rarely = 4; and never = 5.

3. Add up your points for the sixteen questions and look at the interpretation below.

Results

If you had between 72 and 80 points...........................Excellent level of hope

Between 64 and 71 points......................................A very high level of hope

Between 56 and 63 points..Average level of hope

Between 48 and 55 points...Low level of hope

Fewer than 48 points ....Very low level of hope

1. M. Pereyra, "Test de Esperanza-Desesperanza," *Manual del TED y TED-R* (México, DF: Manual Moderno, 2013).

2. M. Sánchez, "Esperanza y satisfacción conyugal en un estudio comparativo entre adventistas y no adventistas" (Tesis de licenciatura de la Facultad de Psicología, de la Universidad de Montemorelos, 2015).

3. T. V. Peraza, "Validación del Test Esperanza-Desesperanza Revisado (TED-R) de Pereyra" (Tesis de Maestría en Relaciones Familiares, Facultad de Educación, Universidad de Montemorelos, 2011).

4. A. Gatti, "Compasión, esperanza-desesperanza y salud mental en adultos jóvenes" (Tesis de licenciatura de la Facultad de Humanidades, Educación y Ciencias Sociales, de la Universidad Adventista del Plata, 2015).

5. Peraza, "Validación del Test Esperanza-Desesperanza Revisado (TED-R) de Pereyra."

6. J. Alcántara, "Calidad de vida, esperanza y religiosidad intrínseca en personas de tercera edad de Montemorelos" (Tesis de Maestría de la Universidad de Montemorelos, 2013).

7. Pereyra, "Test de Esperanza-Desesperanza."